Instant Pot Cookbook For Two

101 Amazingly Fast, Simple & Flavorful Recipes Made For Your Instant Pot Electric Pressure Cooker

By Jason Pacha

Table of Contents

Introduction...**9**

Chapter 1: Instant Pot 101...**11**

The Instant Pot and its Benefits...11

How Does the Instant Pot Work?...12

Instant Pot Control Panel...12

How to Choose a Good Instant Pot......................................14

IP-DUO60..14

IP-DUO Plus60..14

IP-DUO50..14

IP-DUO80..14

IP-LUX60 V3..14

IP-Smart Bluetooth..15

Dos and Don'ts of Instant Pot..15

Chapter 2: Delicious Soups, Stews, and Chilies.............**17**

1. Classy Creamy Mushroom Stew.....................................17

2. Divine Cabbage Beef Soup...18

3. Creamy Garlic Chicken Noodle Soup..............................19

4. Amazing Spinach, Kale, and Artichoke Soup..................20

5. Exquisite Chicken Avocado Soup....................................21

6. Deluxe Cauliflower Stew...22

7. Elegant Cauliflower and Cheddar Soup..........................23

8. Savory Beef and Squash Stew..24

9. Smoky Bacon Chili..25

10. Weeknight Clam Chowder...26

11. Enriching Lamb Stew..27

12. Almost-Famous Chicken Chili.......................................28

13. Delicious Broccoli Cheese Soup...29

14. Tongue-Kicking Jalapeno Popper Soup..30

15. Southwestern Pork Stew..31

16. Spiced Pumpkin and Sausage Soup..32

17. Autumn Beef and Vegetable Stew..33

18. Splendid Broccoli and Ham Chowder..34

19. Magnificent Asparagus Stew...35

20. Satisfying Turkey Stew...36

Chapter 3: Flavored Beef, Pork, and Lamb......................................37

21. Killer Baby Back Ribs..37

22. Juicy Brisket..38

23. Contest-Winning Lamb Curry..39

24. Flavorsome Pulled Pork..40

25. Super Yummy Pork Chops...41

26. Hearty Lemon & Garlic Pork..42

27. Tasty Thai Beef...43

28. Flavorful Beef and Tomato Stuffed Squash..................................44

29. Gratifying Meatloaf..45

30. Lavender Lamb Chops...46

31. Lovely Ginger Beef and Kale..47

32. Extraordinary Pork Roast..48

33. Remarkable Apple Cider Pork Loin...49

34. Awe-Inspiring Lamb Roast..50

35. Melt-in-Your-Mouth Salisbury Steak...51

Chapter 4: Mouthwatering Seafood and Chicken..............................52

36. Spicy Spirited Lemon Salmon...52

37. Awesome Coconut Shrimp Curry...53

38. Wondrous Mediterranean Fish...54

39. Wild Alaskan Cod...55

40. Stunning Shrimp and Sausage Gumbo...56

41. Appetizing Steamed Crab Legs...57

42. Mouthwatering Parmesan Cod..58

43. Lovely Tilapia Fillets..59

44. Generous Orange Trout Fillets...60

45. Intriguing Oysters...61

46. Robust Halibut Fillets..62

47. Fantastic Chili Lime Cod..63

48. Delicious Cauliflower Risotto and Salmon..64

49. Tender Ginger Sesame Glaze Salmon...65

50. Supreme Chicken Breasts...66

51. Delicious Cheesy Spinach Stuffed Chicken Breasts.............................67

52. Royal Lemon Pepper Chicken..68

53. Flaming Buffalo Chicken Strips..69

54. Succulent Garlic Paprika Chicken Legs with Green Beans...................70

55. Phenomenal Whole Rotisserie Chicken...71

Chapter 5: Vegan and Vegetarian...72

56. Unbelievable Zucchini with Avocado Sauce..72

57. Awesome Vegan Patties..73

58. Scrumptious Brussels Sprouts..74

59. Wonderful Eggplant Lasagna...75

60. Won't Know it's Vegan Chili..76

61. Buddha's Tofu and Broccoli Delight...77

62. Special Spicy Almond Tofu..78

63. Fresh Garlic Cauliflower and Sweet Potato Mash...............................79

64. Everyday Bold Beet and Caper Salad....................................80

65. Fragrant Zucchini Mix....................................81

66. Not Your Average Mushroom Risotto....................................82

Chapter 6: Side Dishes, Stocks, and Sauces....................................83

67. Ultimate Corn on the Cob....................................83

68. Tangy Steamed Artichokes....................................84

69. Succulent Sausage and Cheese Dip....................................85

70. Zesty Onion and Cauliflower Dip....................................86

71. Ravishing Mushrooms and Sausage Gravy....................................87

72. Flawless Cranberry Sauce....................................88

73. Perfect Marinara Sauce....................................89

74. Very Cheesy Cheese Sauce....................................90

75. Best Homemade Alfredo Sauce....................................91

76. Hot Dogs with a Twist....................................92

77. Knockout Asparagus and Shrimp Mix....................................93

78. Heavenly Stuffed Bell Peppers....................................94

79. Delicious Broccoli and Garlic Combo....................................95

80. Hollywood Collard Greens and Bacon....................................96

81. Godly Kale Delish....................................97

Chapter 7: Festival & Weekend Recipes....................................98

82. Authentic Indian Butter Chicken....................................98

83. Rockstar Chicken Wings....................................99

84. Festive Okra Pilaf....................................100

Chapter 8: Special Occasion Recipes....................................101

85. Thankful Thanksgiving Whole Turkey....................................101

86. Luscious Broccoli and Asparagus with Roasted Almonds....................................102

87. Yummy Mango Puree....................................103

88. Crunchy Pumpkin Pie...104

Chapter 9: Amazing Desserts...105

89. Delectable Brownie Cake...105

90. Healthy Corn Pudding...106

91. Lovely Cinnamon Baked Apples...107

92. Delicious Peach Cobbler..108

93. Creamy Chocolate Pudding...109

94. Just as Filling Cauliflower Rice Pudding..110

95. Almost-Famous Chocolate Lava Cake...111

96. Irresistible Lemon Cheesecake...112

97. Berry Bliss Cheesecake...113

98. Fantastic Bread Pudding...114

Chapter 10: Wicked Recipes 115

99. Fabulous Goose Meat...115

100. Nourishing Jambalaya...116

101. Party Octopus...117

Conclusion...118

Introduction

Greetings! Jason Pacha here. Firstly, I would like to congratulate and thank you for choosing this book, **"Instant Pot Cookbook For Two- 101 Amazingly Fast, Simple & Flavorful Recipes Made For Your Instant Pot Electric Pressure Cooker"**.

How often you don't have time to prepare a meal? Do you just want to put all the ingredients into an instant pot, wait for the cooking process to end, and have delectable dinner in a few minutes? Do you often just cook for two? Keep reading, you will find all the answers in this book!

Instant Pot is a revolutionary multi-cooker that cooks foods in a matter of minutes. This book is a complete guide of Instant Pot cooking. You will learn essential knowledge about the Instant Pot using, such as:

1. **What Is An Instant Pot.**
2. **How An Instant Pot Work.**
3. **Benefits of Using Instant Pot**
4. **How To Choose An Instant Pot**
5. **Dos and Don'ts of Instant Pot**
6. **Other Useful Advice And More!**

After learning about the Instant Pot using, this book will open the splendid world of flavorsome foods to you. We have collected over 100 easy recipes, which all are well-chosen and chef-proved. Most of the recipes are low in carbohydrates and can reduce weight. With 101 **recipes**, you certainly have a new meal everyday for the next few weeks.

All the recipes are unique, delicious, easy to make, and with ingredients that are inexpensive. Consider this book not just your average cookbook but as your best friend.

This book is created for daily use; it contains a multitude of healthy and wonderful recipes you can enjoy each day.

We have made this book very easy to follow. The tips and essential knowledge of the Instant Pot are just a few minutes of reading. This book is not just a good guide for your Instant Pot, we believe it will be your lifelong companion. The next few weeks will be full of amazing results.

But please be noted, although this book title is Instant Pot Cookbook For Two, it is also suitable for single or family with many individuals. The serves in recipes may not 2, but you can adjust the portion or quantity of ingredients accordingly. As different people have different eating amount. Wish you will have your favorite dishes by this Instant Pot Cookbook!

Chapter 1: Instant Pot 101

The Instant Pot is a revolutionary multi-cooker that cooks foods in a matter of minutes. The pressure cooker uses both pressure and heat to cook your foods through. The multi-cooker also retains the nutrients from your pressure-cooked meals, because it steams food quickly and evenly. In this chapter, you will learn everything about the Instant Pot and discover how to use it like a professional.

The Instant Pot and its Benefits

The Instant Pot is a multi-cooker, designed to prepare a variety of meals quickly and deliciously. With an Instant Pot, you can pressure cook, slow cook, sauté, make yogurt, cook rice, and more, and this can be accomplished by pressing a couple of buttons and letting the machine do the rest. Most modules also come with an automatic shut-off button, so your food will not overcook once ready. The instant pot also has other ample benefits, including:

The Instant Pot cooks foods faster.

An instant pot uses pressure and heat; it will take a much shorter time to cook foods through completely. For example, if you use an oven to bake a chicken, it may take an hour. However, with an Instant Pot, you may only need 20 minutes or less to do the same job.

The Instant Pot retains vitamins and minerals.

Pressure-cooking allows you to retain more vitamins and minerals, as opposed to boiling and steaming your vegetables. The longer you cook, the more nutrition is lost from your food, for vegetables in particular. Since the Instant Pot takes a matter of minutes to cook, everything will retain most of its vitamins and minerals needed to fuel your body.

Moreover, pressure cooking can make foods easier to digest, such as beans and lentils. You can cook foods in the Instant Pot without worrying about having an upset stomach.

The Instant Pot is easy to use.

You need to pay attention when you cook on the stovetop or in the oven, to be sure you don't ruin the meal. The Instant Pot is effortless to use; add all the the ingredients and allow the machine do the rest.

The Instant Pot needs nothing else.

An Instant Pot is the only kitchen appliance you need. With the Instant Pot you can cook a breakfast, lunch, dinner, and dessert. In addition, this book divulges an abundant amount of ketogenic instant pot recipes.

Considering that, the Instant Pot is so easy to clean; remove the gasket from the cover and wash it with warm water.

How Does the Instant Pot Work?

The Instant Pot is a fast way to cook appetizing meals through pressure-cooking. This method uses steam sealed in a pressure cooker; it is an airtight cooking pot. By adding water, the pressure will trap the vapors that rise from the liquid. This, in turn, raises the pressure inside the pressure cooker, along with the temperature of the water. With the increase in temperature and pressure, the cooking process speeds up.

It's easy to use an Instant Pot: Add the ingredients into the pot and adjust the settings. Be aware of what these buttons are and what they do when learning how to use an Instant Pot:

Instant Pot Control Panel.

Here we explain in detail about the different controls and sets on the Instant Pot:

Manual: This is the central button. Press the button and manually set the pressure and cooking time.

Sauté: This button allows you to sauté and brown foods. When using this button, you cook with the lid off (enabling you to stir your ingredients). You can adjust the heat from sauté by pressing the normal setting. *Normal* is for regular browning, *More* is for stir-frying, and *Less* is for simmering (such as thickening sauces).

Keep Warm/Cancel: This button cancels any function and turns your Instant Pot off. When your cooking completes, the Instant Pot will automatically enter a *keep warm* mode and stay there for up to 10 hours. You can cancel the function at any time.

Timer: This button is for delayed cooking. You first need to select a cooking function and make any required adjustments. You can then adjust the timer button using the +/- buttons.

Slow Cook: Pressing this button turns your Instant Pot into a slow cooker.

Pressure: When you cook in *Manual* button, this button will adjust your pressure to low, medium, or high.

Yogurt: Pressing this button allows your Instant Pot to make yogurt.

Soup: This button automatically sets your Instant Pot to high pressure for 30 minutes. Adjust the settings to select a shorter or longer cooking time.

Meat/Stew: This button automatically sets your Instant Pot to high pressure for 35 minutes.

Bean/Chili: This button automatically sets your Instant Pot to high pressure for 30 minutes.

Poultry: This button automatically sets your Instant Pot to high pressure for 15 minutes.

Rice: This button automatically sets your Instant Pot to low pressure and cooks rice based on the amount of water in the pot.

Multi-Grain: This button automatically sets your Instant Pot to high pressure for 40 minutes.

Porridge: This button automatically sets your Instant Pot to high pressure for 20 minutes.

Steam: This button automatically sets your Instant Pot to high for 10 minutes.

When you use a pressure cooker, learn how to release the pressure. With the Instant Pot, it can be done in two ways; either through natural release or quick-release. The natural release allows pressure to release on its own. The quick-release is when you turn the valve on the top from the 'sealing' setting to the 'venting' setting.

How to Choose a Good Instant Pot

There are various versions of the Instant Pot available in the market. Nevertheless, which is the best one for you? From the most popular 6-quart version to larger and more advanced varieties. Here are af few to consider when choosing an Instant Pot:

IP-DUO60.

This is the most popular model of the Instant Pot. This 7-in-1 multifunctional countertop appliance combines a pressure cooker, slow cooker, rice cooker, yogurt maker, steamer, warmer, and sauté/browning functionality.

IP-DUO Plus60.

The Plus 60 is an upgrade to the regular IP-DUO60. It includes more settings, such as the *Cake, Egg,* and *Sterilize* buttons. The alarm clock on this Instant Pot is a blue LCD screen. The Instant Pot's inner bowl also has more comprehensive max/min fill lines.

IP-DUO50.

This Instant Pot holds 5-quarts.

IP-DUO80.

This Instant Pot has a capacity of 8-quarts. It is pricier than the others are, but the extra space might be useful.

IP-LUX60 V3.

This Instant Pot has cake and egg cook settings in the control panel. However, this Instant Pot does not have the Beans/Chili, Poultry, or Yogurt setting, nor an option to cook on low pressure. It also arrives without some of the accessories seen on other models.

IP-Smart Bluetooth.

This Instant Pot is a 6-quart with all the basic functions, and can connect via Bluetooth to your phone; so you can program and monitor cooking from anywhere using the Instant Pot Smart Cooker app.

Choosing a good Instant Pot should not be complicated. It is also best to purchase a new appliance rather than a used one, as they may have broken buttons and complications.

Dos and Don'ts of Instant Pot

If you just started using an Instant Pot, it will be helpful to find out what you should and not do when using the Instant Pot. Here are some valuable tips for cooking with an Instant Pot:

Don't add ingredients to the Instant Pot without the Inner Pot.

It would be a pain if you were to pour ingredients into your Instant Pot without the Inner Pot. Believe me; this happens a lot. That causes damage and is time-consuming to clean.

Don't press the timer button to set the cooking time.

People often mistake the 'timer' button for setting the cook time, and then wonder why the Instant Pot isn't working. Be sure the 'timer' button is not lit before you leave.

Don't overfill your instant pot.

New users frequently fill their Instant Pot with too much food and liquid, which risks clogging the venting knob. To make certain you never overfill, establish that you never pass the max line indicated on the inner pot.

Don't use quick-release for foamy foods or when your Instant Pot is overfilled.

Many new users are confused when it comes to Quick Pressure Release and Natural Pressure Release. If you use Quick-Release when cooking foamy foods, such as grains, beans, or applesauce, it could splatter everywhere. To prevent this from happening, use natural release or release the pressure gradually.

Pay attention to cooking times.

While cooking times for a recipe is a great indicator of the amount of time it takes for your food to cook, the actual cooking time can vary. It is due to the different ingredients and the situations. For example, various meats will take dissimilar times to soften up. To make sure the foods are cooked thouroughly, do not rush through the recipe and mind the end result. Test a small piece from the recipe to asssure that it is done before removing it completely from your Instant Pot.

Read all the instructions carefully.

When you purchase your Instant Pot, read all the instructions carefully to prevent any damages, mishaps, and to be sure that nobody gets hurt.

Inspect your Instant Pot warily.

It is important you keep your instant pot extremely clean so it remains a reliable appliance and in working condition. If parts on your pressure cooker begin to wear out, replace them with original parts, or you risk permanently damaging the appliance.

Clean your Instant Pot.

As previously mentioned, always clean and take care of your Instant Pot to ensure it is in optimal condition. After cooking with your Instant Pot, remove the inner pot and wash it with warm soapy water. Then, use a clean dishrag to wipe the outer parts of the pressure cooker.

Chapter 2: Delicious Soups, Stews, and Chilies

1. Classy Creamy Mushroom Stew

Time: 40 minutes

Servings: 6

Ingredients:

- 1 pound cremini mushrooms, sliced
- 1 celery stalk, chopped
- 2 Tablespoons green onions, chopped
- 2 garlic cloves, minced
- 2 cups beef stock
- ½ cup heavy cream
- 5 ounces cream cheese, softened
- 1 Tablespoon unsalted butter, melted
- 1 Tablespoon lemon juice
- 1 teaspoon fresh or dried thyme
- 2 Tablespoons fresh sage, chopped
- 1 bay leaf
- 1 teaspoon salt
- 1 teaspoon fresh ground black pepper

Instructions:

1. Rinse the mushrooms, pat dry.
2. Press Sauté button on Instant Pot. Melt the butter.
3. Add green onions, garlic. Cook for 1 minute.
4. Add mushrooms, celery, and garlic. Sauté until vegetables are softened.
5. Press Keep Warm/Cancel setting to stop Sauté mode.
6. Add remaining ingredients. Stir well.
7. Close and seal lid. Select Meat/Stew button. Set cooking time to 20 minutes.
8. Once done, Instant Pot will switch to Keep Warm mode.
9. Remain on Keep Warm for 10 minutes.
10. When done, use Quick-Release setting; turn valve from sealing to venting to release pressure quickly. Open the lid with care. Stir ingredients.
11. Serve. Garnish with green onion, grated parmesan cheese.

Nutritional Information:

Calories: 150, Fat: 13g, Protein: 7g, Carbohydrates: 6g, Dietary Fiber: 1.5g

2. Divine Cabbage Beef Soup

Time: 40 minutes

Servings: 6

Ingredients:

- 1 pound lean ground beef
- 1 head green cabbage, chopped
- 1 head red cabbage, chopped
- 1 celery stalk, chopped
- 1 can (28-ounce) diced tomatoes
- 3 cups water
- 1 teaspoon salt
- 1 teaspoon fresh ground black pepper
- 1 Tablespoon fresh parsley, chopped

Instructions:

1. Press Sauté button on Instant Pot.
2. Add ground beef. Sauté until no longer pink; drain.
3. Press Keep Warm/Cancel setting to stop Sauté mode.
4. Return ground beef to Instant Pot. Add cabbage, celery, diced tomatoes, water, parsley, salt, and pepper. Stir well.
5. Close and seal lid. Press Meat/Stew. Cook on High Pressure for 20 minutes.
6. Once done, Instant Pot will switch to Keep Warm mode.
7. Remain in Keep Warm mode for 10 minutes.
8. When done, use Quick-Release. Open the lid with care. Stir ingredients.
9. Serve. Garnish with fresh parsley.

Nutritional Information per serving:

Calories: 115, Fat: 4.4g, Carbohydrates: 11g, Dietary Fiber: 3g, Protein: 11g

3. Creamy Garlic Chicken Noodle Soup

Time: 40 minutes

Servings: 4

Ingredients:

- 1 pound chicken breasts, boneless, skinless
- 1 pound squash noodle spirals (or any keto-friendly alternative)
- 1 celery stalk, chopped
- 1 cup carrots, chopped
- 2 green onions, chopped
- 6 cups chicken broth
- 2 Tablespoons coconut oil
- 1 teaspoon salt (to taste)
- 1 teaspoon fresh ground black pepper)

Instructions:

1. Rinse the chicken, pat dry.
2. Press the Sauté button on your Instant Pot. Heat the coconut oil.
3. Add chicken breasts. Sauté until brown on both sides and cooked through.
4. Remove chicken and shred with a fork.
5. Add celery, carrots, and green onion to Instant Pot. Sauté for 3 minutes.
6. Press Keep Warm/Cancel setting to stop Sauté mode.
7. Return shredded chicken and remaining ingredients to Instant Pot. Stir well.
8. Close and seal lid. Press Soup button. Cook for 30 minutes.
9. When done, set to quick pressure release to vent steam. Open the lid with care. Stir.
10. Spoon into serving bowls. Garnish with fresh green onions.

Nutritional Information per serving:

Calories: 325, Fat: 16g, Carbohydrates: 9g, Dietary Fiber: 3g, Protein: 36g

4. Amazing Spinach, Kale, and Artichoke Soup

Time: 25 minutes

Servings: 4

Ingredients:

- 1 bunch of kale, stemmed and chopped
- 4 cups spinach
- 1-ounce jar artichoke hearts, drained and chopped
- 4 cups low-sodium chicken broth
- ¼ cup cheddar cheese, shredded
- ¼ cup mozzarella cheese, shredded
- 1 Tablespoon butter, melted
- 1 Tablespoon Italian seasoning
- 2 teaspoons fresh parsley, chopped
- 1 teaspoon salt
- 1 teaspoon fresh ground black pepper

Instructions:

1. Place all ingredients in Instant Pot. Stir well.
2. Close and seal lid. Press Manual setting. Cook for 15 minutes.
3. When done, use Quick-Release setting. Open the lid with care. Stir ingredients.
4. Serve.

Nutritional Information per serving:

Calories: 80, Fat: 8g, Carbohydrates, 3g, Protein: 9g, Dietary Fiber: 3g

5. Exquisite Chicken Avocado Soup

Time: 40 minutes

Servings: 4

Ingredients:

- 4 chicken breasts, boneless, skinless
- 1 tablespoon coconut oil
- 4 avocados, peeled and chopped
- 4 cups chicken broth
- Zest and juice from 1 lime
- 1 Tablespoon fresh cilantro, chopped
- 1 teaspoon salt
- 1 teaspoon fresh ground black pepper
- 2 tomatoes, chopped
- 2 garlic cloves, minced

Instructions:

1. Rinse the chicken, pat dry. Cut into strips.
2. Press Sauté button on Instant Pot. Melt the coconut oil.
3. Add chicken strips. Sauté until chicken no longer pink.
4. Add garlic and tomatoes. Stir well.
5. Press Keep Warm/Cancel setting to stop Sauté mode.
6. Add chopped avocados, chicken broth, lime juice, lime zest, cilantro, salt, and black pepper. Stir well.
7. Close and seal lid. Press Meat/Stew button on Instant Pot. Cook for 20 minutes. Once done, Instant Pot will switch to Keep Warm mode.
8. Remain in Keep Warm mode for 10 minutes.
9. When done, use Quick-Release. Open the lid with care. Stir ingredients. Serve.

Nutritional Information per serving:

Calories: 300, Fat: 20g, Protein: 20g, Dietary Fiber: 3g, Carbohydrates: 9g

6. Deluxe Cauliflower Stew

Time: 40 minutes

Servings: 4

Ingredients:

- 4 slices of bacon, cooked and crumbled
- 1 teaspoon coconut oil
- 1 head cauliflower, chopped into florets
- ¼ cup coconut flour
- 4 cups chicken broth
- 2 celery stalks, chopped
- 1 shallot, chopped
- 2 garlic cloves, minced
- 1 teaspoon salt
- 1 teaspoon fresh ground black pepper
- 1 Tablespoon fresh parsley, chopped

Instructions:

1. In a skillet or your Instant Pot, cook the bacon. Drain on paper towel. Set aside.
2. Press Sauté button on Instant Pot. Heat coconut oil.
3. Add cauliflower, celery, shallots, and garlic cloves. Sauté until vegetables soften.
4. Press Keep Warm/Cancel setting to stop Sauté mode.
5. Add coconut flour to ingredients. Stir well. Add chicken broth. Stir well.
6. Close and seal lid. Press Soup button. Cook 30 minutes.
7. When done, set to quick pressure release. Open the lid with care. Stir ingredients.
8. Serve. Garnish with fresh parsley.

Nutritional Information per serving:

Calories: 210, Fat: 16g, Carbohydrates: 7g, Dietary Fiber: 3g, Protein: 10g

7. Elegant Cauliflower and Cheddar Soup

Time: 50 minutes

Servings: 4

Ingredients:

- 2 Tablespoons butter
- 1 head cauliflower, chopped into florets
- 4 cups vegetable broth
- 1 red onion, diced
- 2 garlic cloves, minced
- ½ cup heavy cream
- ½ cup cheddar cheese, grated
- 1 teaspoon salt
- 1 teaspoon fresh ground black pepper

Instructions:

1. Press Sauté button on Instant Pot. Melt the butter.
2. Add red onion, garlic. Sweat for 1 minute.
3. Add cauliflower. Sauté until cauliflower softens.
4. Press Keep Warm/Cancel setting to stop Sauté mode.
5. Add remaining ingredients. Mix well.
6. Close and seal lid. Press Soup button. Cook on high pressure for 30 minutes.
7. When done, Instant Pot will switch to Keep Warm mode.
8. Remain in Keep Warm mode for 10 minutes.
9. When done, use Quick-Release setting. Open the lid with care. Stir ingredients.
10. Serve.

Nutritional Information per serving:

Calories: 120, Fat: 10g, Protein: 6g, Carbohydrates: 5g, Dietary Fiber: 4g

8. Savory Beef and Squash Stew

Time: 50 minutes

Servings: 4

Ingredients:

- 1 pound lean ground beef
- 2 pounds butternut squash, peeled, chopped into chunks
- 1 (6-ounce) can sliced mushrooms
- 2 Tablespoons butter
- 4 cups beef broth
- 1 red onion, diced
- 2 garlic cloves, minced
- 1 teaspoon fresh rosemary, chopped
- 2 teaspoons paprika
- 1 teaspoon salt (to taste)
- 1 teaspoon fresh ground black pepper (to taste)

Instructions:

1. Press Sauté button on Instant Pot. Melt the butter.
2. Sauté the onions, garlic for 1 minute.
3. Add ground beef, butternut squash, and mushrooms.
4. Sauté until the ground beef is no longer pink and vegetables soften.
5. Press Keep Warm/Cancel setting to stop Sauté mode.
6. Add beef stock, rosemary, paprika, salt, and black pepper. Mix well.
7. Close and seal lid. Press Soup button. Cook on high pressure for 30 minutes.
8. After 30 minutes, Instant Pot will switch to Keep Warm.
9. Remain in Keep Warm 10 minutes.
10. When done, use Quick-Release. Open the lid with care. Stir ingredients.
11. Serve.

Nutritional Information per serving:

Calories: 245, Fat, 7g, Protein: 25g, Carbohydrates: 15g, Dietary Fiber: 8g

9. Smoky Bacon Chili

Time: 40 minutes   Servings: 4

Ingredients:

- 8 slices bacon, cooked and crumbled
- 2 pounds lean ground beef
- 1 can (6-ounce) tomato paste
- 1 can (14-ounce) diced tomatoes
- 1 yellow onion, chopped
- 2 garlic cloves, minced
- 1 yellow bell pepper, chopped
- 1 red bell pepper, chopped
- 1 green bell pepper, chopped
- 2 Tablespoons fresh cilantro, chopped
- 1 Tablespoon smoked paprika
- 1 Tablespoon chili powder
- 2 teaspoons cumin
- 1 teaspoon salt (to taste)
- 1 teaspoon fresh ground black pepper (to taste)

Instructions:

1. Press Sauté button on Instant Pot. Add ground beef.
2. Cook until brown. Drain, and set aside.
3. Drizzle 1 teaspoon coconut oil along bottom of Instant Pot. Add yellow onion, garlic cloves. Cook 1 minute. Add the bell peppers. Sauté until tender to a fork.
4. Press Keep Warm/Cancel setting to stop Sauté mode.
5. Return ground beef, remaining ingredients, seasoning to Instant Pot. Stir well.
6. Close and seal lid. Press Bean/Chili button. Cook for 30 minutes.
7. Once done, naturally release or quick-release pressure. Open the lid with care. Stir ingredients. (Add more seasoning if desired.). Serve.

Nutritional Information per serving:

Calories: 400, Fat: 35g, Carbohydrates, 13g, Dietary Fiber: 4g, Protein: 32g

10. Weeknight Clam Chowder

Time: 45 minutes

Servings: 4

Ingredients:

- 3 (10-ounce) cans fancy whole baby clams
- 1 pound bacon strips, cooked and crumbled
- 1 Tablespoon butter
- 2 cups chicken broth
- 2 cups heavy cream
- 4 garlic cloves, minced
- 1 red onion, chopped
- 8 ounce package cream cheese
- ¼ cup mozzarella cheese, shredded
- 1 teaspoon ground thyme
- 2 teaspoons salt (to taste)
- 1 teaspoon fresh ground black pepper (to taste)

Instructions:

1. Press Sauté button on Instant Pot. Melt the butter.
2. Add red onion and garlic. Cook/sweat 1 minute.
3. Press Keep Warm/Cancel setting to stop Sauté mode.
4. Add remaining ingredients. Stir well.
5. Close and seal lid. Press Manual setting. Cook on high pressure 30 minutes.
6. Once done, Instant Pot will switch to Keep Warm mode.
7. Remain in Keep Warm mode 5 minutes.
8. Naturally release or quick-release the pressure. Open the lid with care. Stir.
9. Serve.

Nutritional Information per serving:

Calories: 250, Fat: 30g, Protein: 12g, Carbohydrates: 3g, Dietary Fiber: 2g

11. Enriching Lamb Stew

Time: 45 minutes

Servings: 4

Ingredients:

- 2 pounds lamb shoulder
- 1 Tablespoon butter
- 1 red onion, chopped
- 4 garlic cloves, minced
- 2 tomatoes, diced
- 3 cups vegetable broth
- 1 (14-ounce) can coconut milk
- 1 teaspoon ginger, grated
- 1 Tablespoon fresh cilantro, chopped
- 1 teaspoon salt
- 1 teaspoon fresh ground black pepper

Instructions:

1. Wash the lamb, pat dry. Cut into chunks.
2. Press Sauté button on Instant Pot. Melt the butter.
3. Add red onion, garlic to Instant Pot. Cook/sweat for 1 minute.
4. Add lamb shoulder. Sear (brown) on all sides.
5. Press Keep Warm/Cancel button to stop Sauté mode.
6. Add tomatoes, vegetable stock, coconut milk, ginger, cilantro, salt and pepper. Stir well.
7. Close and seal lid. Press Meat/Stew button. Cook for 35 minutes.
8. Quick-release the pressure when done. Open the lid with care. Stir ingredients.
9. Serve. Garnish with fresh cilantro.

Nutritional Information per serving:

Calories: 300, Fat: 30g, Carbohydrates: 6g, Protein: 48g, Dietary Fiber: 0.5g

12. Almost-Famous Chicken Chili

Time: 40 minutes

Servings: 4

Ingredients:

- 1 pound ground chicken
- 1 Tablespoon butter
- 1 yellow onion, diced
- 2 garlic cloves, minced
- 1 red bell pepper, chopped
- 1 green bell pepper, chopped
- 2 celery stalks, chopped
- 1 jalapeno pepper, chopped (optional)
- 1 cup corn kernels
- 1 can (14-ounce) diced tomatoes
- 2 cups chicken broth
- 1 can (6-ounce) tomato paste
- 1 teaspoon ground cumin
- 1 teaspoon smoked paprika
- 1 Tablespoon fresh cilantro, chopped
- 1 teaspoon salt (to taste)
- 1 teaspoon fresh ground black pepper (to taste)

Instructions:

1. Press Sauté button on Instant Pot. Melt the butter.
2. Add onions and garlic. Sweat for 1 minute.
3. Add ground chicken. Sauté until chicken is brown.
4. Add red and green bell peppers, celery, jalapeno, corn, tomatoes. Stir well.
5. Add tomato paste. Stir well. Add chicken broth. Stir well.
6. Add the spices. Stir well.
7. Press Keep Warm/Cancel setting to stop Sauté mode.
8. Close and seal lid. Press Bean/Chili button. Cook for 30 minutes.
9. Naturally release or quick-release pressure once done. Stir ingredients.
10. Serve.

Nutritional Information per serving:

Calories: 225, Fat: 8g, Carbohydrates: 20g, Protein: 20g, Dietary Fiber: 6g

13. Delicious Broccoli Cheese Soup

Time: 40 minutes

Servings: 4

Ingredients:

- 1 head broccoli, chopped into florets
- 4 garlic cloves, minced
- 3 cups vegetable broth
- 1 cup heavy cream
- 3 cups cheddar cheese, shredded
- 1 teaspoon salt (to taste)
- 1 teaspoon fresh ground black pepper (to taste)

Instructions:

1. In your Instant Pot, add broccoli florets, garlic, vegetable stock, heavy cream, and shredded cheese. Stir well.
2. Close and seal lid. Press Soup button. Cook for 30 minutes.
3. Naturally release or quick-release pressure when done. Open the lid with care. Stir.
4. Serve.

Nutritional Information per serving:

Calories: 250, Fat: 25g, Carbohydrates: 5g, Dietary Fiber: 1g, Protein: 14g

14. Tongue-Kicking Jalapeno Popper Soup

Time: 40 minutes   Servings: 4

Ingredients:

- 2 chicken breasts, boneless, skinless
- 2 Tablespoons coconut oil
- 6 slices of bacon, cooked and crumbled
- 4 jalapeno peppers, finely sliced
(depending on desired heat level, can leave some seeds in, or remove all the seeds)
- 2 Tablespoons butter
- ½ cup cream cheese, softened
- 1 cup heavy cream
- 2 cups chicken broth
- 2 Tablespoons salsa verde (or green sauce)
- ½ cup cheddar cheese, shredded
- ½ cup mozzarella cheese, shredded
- 1 teaspoon garlic powder
- 1 teaspoon salt (to taste)
- 1 teaspoon black pepper (to taste)

Instructions:

1. Rinse the chicken, pat dry.
2. Press Sauté button on Instant Pot. Heat the coconut oil. Add chicken breasts.
3. Cook until chicken breasts cooked through. Remove and shred chicken with fork.
4. Press Keep Warm/Cancel button to stop Sauté mode.
5. Return chicken to Instant Pot. Add rest of ingredients. Stir well.
6. Close and seal lid. Press Soup button. Cook 30 minutes.
7. Naturally or quick-release pressure when the timer beeps,. Open the lid with care. Stir.
8. Serve.

Nutritional Information per serving:

Calories: 300, Fat: 38g, Carbohydrates: 2g, Protein: 17g, Dietary Fiber: 1.2g

15. Southwestern Pork Stew

Time: 40 minutes

Servings: 4

Ingredients:

- 1 pound pork shoulder
- 1 red onion, diced
- 2 garlic cloves, minced
- 2 Tablespoons coconut oil
- 6-ounce can sliced mushrooms
- 1 green bell pepper, chopped
- 1 red bell pepper, chopped
- 4 cups beef broth
- Juice from 1 lime
- ½ cup tomato paste
- 2 teaspoons chili powder
- 2 teaspoons ground cumin
- 1 Tablespoon fresh cilantro, chopped
- 1 teaspoon smoked paprika
- 1 teaspoon salt (to taste)
- 1 teaspoon fresh ground black pepper (to taste)

Instructions:

1. Rinse the pork shoulder, pat dry. Cut into chunks.
2. Press Sauté button on Instant Pot. Heat the coconut oil.
3. Add onion, garlic. Sweat for 1 minute. Add pork shoulder. Brown on all sides.
4. Add mushrooms, bell peppers. Sauté until vegetables have softened.
5. Press Keep Warm/Cancel button to stop Sauté mode.
6. Add rest of ingredients. Stir well.
7. Close and seal lid. Press Soup button. Cook for 30 minutes.
8. When the timer beeps, quick-release or naturally release pressure. Open the lid with care. Stir ingredients.
9. Serve.

Nutritional Information per serving:

Calories: 350, Fat: 28g, Carbohydrates: 10g, Dietary Fiber: 3g, Protein: 20g

16. Spiced Pumpkin and Sausage Soup

Time: 40 minutes

Servings: 4

Ingredients:

- 1 pound pork sausage, chopped
- 2 cups pumpkin puree (not pie filling)
- 2 cups vegetable broth
- 1 cup heavy cream
- 4 Tablespoons butter
- 1 red onion
- 2 garlic cloves, minced
- 4 slices of bacon, cooked and crumbled
- 1 teaspoon onion powder
- 1 teaspoon ground cumin
- 1 teaspoon cinnamon
- 1 teaspoon ginger, grated
- 1 teaspoon salt (to taste)
- 1 teaspoon fresh ground black pepper (to taste)

Instructions:

1. Cook the bacon. Crumble in small pieces and set aside.
2. Press Sauté button on Instant Pot. Melt the butter.
3. Add onion and garlic. Sweat for 1 minute.
4. Add sausage. Sauté until sausage is brown.
5. Add pumpkin puree. Stir well.
6. Add vegetable stock, heavy cream. Stir well.
7. Add seasoning. Stir well.
8. Press Keep Warm/Cancel setting to stop Sauté mode.
9. Close and seal lid. Press Soup button. Cook for 30 minutes.
10. Quick-release or naturally release pressure when done. Open the lid with care. Stir.
11. Top with crumbled bacon. Serve.

Nutritional Information per serving:

Calories: 125, Fat: 10g, Carbohydrates: 10g, Protein: 5g, Dietary Fiber: 5g

17. Autumn Beef and Vegetable Stew

Time: 45 minutes   Servings: 4

Ingredients:

- 1½ pounds stewing beef chunks
- 4 zucchini, chopped
- 2 carrots, chopped
- 2 cups frozen peas
- 4 cups vegetable broth
- 1 Tablespoon coconut oil
- ½ cup ghee
- 1 red onion, chopped
- 4 garlic cloves, minced
- 2 tomatoes, chopped
- 2 Tablespoons ground cumin
- 1 Tablespoon ground ginger
- 1 teaspoon salt (to taste)
- 1 teaspoon fresh ground black pepper (to taste)

Instructions:

1. Press Sauté button on Instant Pot. Heat the coconut oil.
2. Add onions and garlic. Sweat for 1 minute.
3. Add stewing beef. Brown on all sides. Add zucchini, carrots, and peas.
4. Press Keep Warm/Cancel setting to stop Sauté mode.
5. Add ghee. Stir well. Add vegetable stock. Stir well. Add tomatoes, cumin, ginger, salt and pepper. Stir well.
6. Close and seal lid. Press Meat/Stew button. Cook for 35 minutes.
7. When the timer beeps, quick-release or naturally release pressure. Open the lid with care. Stir ingredients.
8. Spoon into serving bowls.

Nutritional Information per serving:

Calories: 200, Protein: 31g, Fat: 40g, Carbohydrates: 13, Dietary Fiber: 4g

18. Splendid Broccoli and Ham Chowder

Time: 50 minutes

Servings: 6

Ingredients:

- 1 head of broccoli
- 1 pound of ham
- 2 Tablespoons coconut oil
- 1 celery stalk, chopped
- 1 yellow onion, chopped
- 4 garlic cloves, minced
- 4 cups vegetable broth
- 1 cup of organic heavy cream
- ¼ cup mozzarella cheese, shredded
- ¼ cup parmesan cheese, shredded
- ¼ cup fresh parsley, chopped
- 1 teaspoon salt (to taste)
- 1 teaspoon fresh ground black pepper (to taste)

Instructions:

1. Rinse the broccoli, chop into florets. Chop ham into chunks.
2. Press Sauté button on Instant Pot. Heat the coconut oil.
3. Add onions and garlic. Sweat for 1 minute.
4. Add celery. Add cauliflower and ham.
5. Sauté until meat is brown and vegetables have softened.
6. Press Keep Warm/Cancel button to stop Sauté mode.
7. Add vegetable stock, heavy cream. Stir well.
8. Add mozzarella cheese, parmesan cheese. Stir well.
9. Close and seal lid. Press Manual button. Cook on High Pressure for 30 minutes.
10. Instant Pot will switch to Keep Warm mode when the timer beeps,.
11. Remain on Keep Warm for 10 minutes.
12. Use Quick-Release when done,. Open the lid with care. Stir ingredients.
13. Serve.

Nutritional Information per serving:

Calories: 125, Fat: 7g, Protein: 13g, Carbohydrates: 5g, Dietary Fiber: 2g

19. Magnificent Asparagus Stew

Time: 45 minutes

Servings: 4

Ingredients:

- 2 Tablespoons coconut oil
- 1 pound of asparagus
- 1 green bell pepper, chopped
- 1 red bell pepper, chopped
- 2 shallots, chopped
- 4 garlic cloves, minced
- 1 leek, chopped
- 4 cups vegetable broth
- ¼ cup fresh parsley, chopped
- 1 teaspoon salt (to taste)
- 1 teaspoon fresh ground black pepper (to taste)

Instructions:

1. Rinse asparagus, pat dry.
2. Break off woodsy end. Chop asparagus in bite-size pieces.
3. Press Sauté button on Instant Pot. Heat the coconut oil.
4. Add asparagus, bell peppers, shallots, garlic cloves and leeks.
5. Sauté until vegetables have softened.
6. Press Keep Warm/Cancel setting to stop Sauté mode.
7. Add vegetable broth and parsley. Stir well.
8. Close and seal lid. Press Meat/Stew button on Instant Pot. Cook 35 minutes.
9. Quick release pressure when the timer beeps,. Open the lid with care. Stir ingredients.
10. Serve.

Nutritional Information per serving:

Calories: 90, Carbohydrates: 6.5g, Protein: 6g, Fat: 26g, Dietary Fiber: 9g

20. Satisfying Turkey Stew

Time: 45 minutes

Servings: 4

Ingredients:

- 4 cups cooked turkey meat, cut in chunks (not ground turkey)
- 4 celery stalks, chopped
- 2 green onions, chopped
- 2 garlic cloves, minced
- 4 carrots, chopped
- 4 cups turkey or vegetable broth
- Zest and juice from ½ lemon
- 2 Tablespoons coconut oil
- 1 Tablespoon coconut flour
- 1 teaspoon salt (to taste)
- 1 teaspoon fresh ground black pepper (to taste)

Instructions:

1. Press Sauté button on Instant Pot. Heat the coconut oil.
2. Add green onions and garlic. Sweat for 1 minute.
3. Add celery and carrots. Sauté until vegetables have softened.
4. Press Keep Warm/Cancel button to end Sauté mode.
5. Add turkey. Stir in coconut flour to coat ingredients.
6. Pour in turkey/vegetable broth, lemon juice, lemon zest, salt, and pepper. Stir.
7. Close and seal lid. Press Meat/Stew button. Cook for 35 minutes.
8. When the timer beeps, set to quick pressure release. Open the lid with care. Stir.
9. Spoon into serving bowls. Serve.

Nutritional Information per serving:

Calories: 215, Fat: 4g, Protein: 28g, Carbohydrates: 10g, Dietary Fiber: 0.5g

Chapter 3: Flavored Beef, Pork, and Lamb

21. Killer Baby Back Ribs

Time: 45 minutes   Servings: 4

Ingredients:

- 1 rack baby back ribs
- 2 Tablespoons soy sauce
- 2 cups beef broth
- 2 Tablespoons granulated Splenda
- 2 Tablespoons coconut oil
- 3 Tablespoons fresh ginger, grated
- 4 garlic cloves, minced
- 1 Tablespoon chili powder
- 1 Tablespoon paprika
- 1 teaspoon ground mustard
- 1 teaspoon low-carb brown sugar
- 1 teaspoon cayenne pepper
- 1 teaspoon onion powder
- 1 teaspoon salt (to taste)
- 1 teaspoon fresh ground black pepper (to taste)

Instructions:

1. In a small bowl, combine ginger, chili powder, paprika, ground mustard, cayenne pepper, onion powder, salt and pepper. Stir well.
2. Add Splenda, brown sugar. Stir well.
3. Rinse the ribs. (You want ribs slightly damp so seasoning will cling.)
4. Rub seasoning mix on both sides of ribs. Place on a flat baking sheet.
5. Pre-heat oven to a broil. Place baking sheet under broiler. Broil 5 minutes per side. Press Sauté mode on Instant Pot. Heat coconut oil.
6. Add garlic and ginger. Cook for 1 minute.
7. Add soy sauce and beef broth. Boil for 15 seconds. Stir well.
8. Press Keep Warm/Cancel setting to end Sauté mode.
9. Slice up the rack of ribs into chunks of 4-5 ribs. Place in Instant Pot.
10. Close and seal lid. Press Manual button. Cook on High Pressure for 35 minutes.
11. When done, release the pressure quickly or naturally. Open the lid with care.
12. Serve.

Nutritional Information per serving:

Calories: 500, Fat: 40g, Carbohydrates: 1.5g, Dietary Fiber: 0.9g, Protein: 55g

22. Juicy Brisket

Time: 50 minutes

Servings: 5

Ingredients:

- 2 pounds of brisket
- 2 Tablespoons coconut oil
- 8-ounces low-carb beer
- 2 Tablespoons soy sauce
- 2 Tablespoons Worcestershire sauce
- 1 Tablespoon dry mustard
- 3 Tablespoons tomato paste
- 2 shallots, thinly sliced
- 1 teaspoon of salt (to taste)
- 1 teaspoon fresh ground black pepper (to taste)

Instructions:

1. In a large Ziploc bag, add all the ingredients. Massage the ingredients.
2. Allow to marinate for 2 hours, up to 12 hours.
3. When ready to cook, transfer all ingredients to Instant Pot.
4. Close and seal lid. Press Manual setting. Cook on High Pressure for 40 minutes.
5. Once done, quick-release or naturally release the pressure. Open the lid with care.
6. Press Sauté mode. Cook until all the liquid evaporates.
7. Remove the brisket. Let it rest for 5 – 15 minutes before slicing.
8. Serve and enjoy!

Nutritional Information per serving:

Calories: 400, Fat: 20g, Carbohydrates: 3.5g, Dietary Fiber: 0.5g, Protein: 45g

23. Contest-Winning Lamb Curry

Time: 40 minutes

Servings: 4

Ingredients:

- 1 pound skinless, boneless lamb
- 1 (8-ounce) can diced tomatoes
- 1 Tablespoon fresh ginger, grated
- 4 garlic cloves, minced
- 1 chili, minced
- ½ cup Greek yogurt
- 1 shallot, chopped
- 1 teaspoon ground cumin
- 1 teaspoon turmeric powder
- ¼ cup fresh cilantro, chopped
- 1 teaspoon salt (to taste)
- 1 teaspoon fresh ground black pepper (to taste)

Instructions:

1. Rinse the lamb, pat dry. Cut into chunks.
2. In a large glass dish, combine all the ingredients. Stir well. Cover with plastic wrap. Place glass dish in refrigerator. Allow to marinate for 2 – 8 hours.
3. When ready to cook, transfer lamb mixture to Instant Pot.
4. Close and seal lid. Press Manual button. Cook on High Pressure for 30 minutes.
5. Release pressure naturally when done. Open the lid with care.
6. Press Sauté button and boil until sauce has thickened.
7. Serve.

Nutritional Information per serving:

Calories: 350, Fat: 8g, Dietary Fiber: 2g, Carbohydrates: 15g, Protein: 21g

24. Flavorsome Pulled Pork

Time: 45 minutes

Servings: 4

Ingredients:

- 3 pounds boneless pork shoulder
- 2 Tablespoons coconut oil
- 1 teaspoon onion powder
- 1 teaspoon garlic powder
- 1 Tablespoon paprika
- 1 cup beef broth
- 1 teaspoon salt (to taste)
- 1 teaspoon fresh ground black pepper (to taste)

Barbeque Sauce Ingredients:

- 3 Tablespoons low-sugar ketchup
- 4 Tablespoons granulated Splenda
- ¼ cup yellow mustard
- 2 teaspoons hot sauce
- 3 Tablespoons apple cider vinegar

Instructions:

1. In a small bowl, combine onion powder, garlic powder, paprika, salt and pepper. Mix well. Rub seasoning on pork shoulder.
2. Press Sauté mode on Instant Pot. Heat coconut oil.
3. Sear all sides of pork shoulder.
4. In another bowl, combine barbecue sauce ingredients. Stir well.
5. Press Keep Warm/Cancel setting to end Sauté mode.
6. Add the barbecue sauce and beef broth to Instant Pot. Stir well.
7. Close and seal lid. Press Manual button. Cook on high pressure for 35 minutes.
8. Quick-release or naturally release pressure when done. Open the lid with care.
9. Use two forks to pull pork apart.
10. Press Sauté button. Simmer until sauce reduced and clings to pork.
11. Press Keep Warm/Cancel button.
12. Serve.

Nutritional Information per serving:

Calories: 265, Fat 16g, Carbohydrates: 1g, Protein: 20g, Dietary Fiber: 1.5g

25. Super Yummy Pork Chops

Time: 25 minutes

Servings: 4

Ingredients:

- 4 boneless pork chops
- 2 Tablespoons coconut oil
- 2 cups beef broth
- 4 garlic cloves, minced
- 1 teaspoon nutmeg
- 1 teaspoon paprika
- 1 teaspoon onion powder
- 1 teaspoon salt
- 1 teaspoon fresh ground black pepper

Instructions:

1. Season the pork chops with spices listed.
2. Press Sauté button on Instant Pot. Heat the coconut oil.
3. Sear pork chops for 2 minutes per side.
4. Press Keep Warm/Cancel button to end Sauté mode.
5. Pour in beef broth.
6. Close and seal lid. Press Poultry button on control panel. Cook for 15 minutes.
7. Quick-release the pressure when done. Open the lid with care.
8. Serve.

Nutritional Information per serving:

Calories: 500, Protein: 30g, Carbohydrates: 8g, Dietary Fiber: 1g, Fat: 10g

26. Hearty Lemon & Garlic Pork

Time: 25 minutes

Servings: 4

Ingredients:

- 4 pork chops, boneless
- 2 cups beef broth
- 3 Tablespoons ghee, melted
- 3 Tablespoons coconut oil
- 1 teaspoon salt
- 1 teaspoon fresh ground black pepper
- Zest and juice from 2 lemons
- 6 garlic cloves, minced
- ¼ cup fresh parsley, chopped

Instructions:

1. Season the pork chops with salt and pepper, lemon juice and zest.
2. Press the Sauté button on your Instant Pot. Heat coconut oil.
3. Sauté garlic for 1 minute. Add pork chops. Sear for 2 minutes per side.
4. Press the Keep Warm/Cancel button to end Sauté mode.
5. Add ghee and beef broth to the Instant Pot.
6. Close and seal lid. Press Poultry button. Cook for 15 minutes.
7. Quick-release pressure when done. Open the lid with care. Stir ingredients.
8. Serve.

Nutritional Information per serving:

Calories: 425, Fat: 25g, Dietary Fiber: 1g, Carbohydrates: 6g, Protein: 40g

27. Tasty Thai Beef

Time: 30 minutes

Servings: 6

Ingredients:

- 1 pound of beef, cut into strips
- 1 green bell pepper, chopped
- 1 red bell pepper, chopped
- Zest and juice from 1 lemon
- 2 cups beef broth
- 2 teaspoons ginger, grated
- 4 garlic cloves, minced
- 2 Tablespoons coconut oil
- 1 Tablespoon coconut amino
- 1 cup roasted pecans
- 1 teaspoon salt
- 1 teaspoon fresh ground black pepper

Instructions:

1. Press Sauté button on Instant Pot. Heat the coconut oil.
2. Sauté garlic and ginger for 1 minute.
3. Add beef strips. Sear 1-2 minutes per side.
4. Add bell peppers. Add salt and pepper.
5. Continue cooking until meat is no longer pink.
6. Add coconut amino, pecans, zest and juice from lemon, beef broth. Stir well.
7. Close and seal lid. Press Manual setting. Cook at High Pressure for 15 minutes.
8. Release pressure naturally when done. Open the lid with care.
9. Let it sit for 5 – 10 minutes.
10. Serve.

Nutritional Information per serving:

Calories: 225, Fat: 15g, Dietary Fiber: 1g, Carbohydrates: 3g, Protein: 20g

28. Flavorful Beef and Tomato Stuffed Squash

Time: 30 minutes

Servings: 4

Ingredients:

- 1 pound of beef, chopped into chunks
- 1 pound butternut squash, peeled and chopped
- 2 Tablespoons coconut oil
- 2 Tablespoons ghee, melted
- 1 green bell pepper, chopped
- 1 yellow bell pepper, chopped
- 2 (14-ounce) cans diced tomatoes
- 4 garlic cloves, minced
- 1 yellow or red onion, chopped
- 1 Tablespoon fresh thyme, chopped
- 1 Tablespoon fresh rosemary, chopped
- 2 Tablespoons fresh parsley, chopped
- 1 teaspoon cayenne pepper
- 1 teaspoon salt
- 1 teaspoon fresh ground black pepper

Instructions:

1. Press Sauté button on Instant Pot. Heat the coconut oil.
2. Add onion and garlic. Sweat for 2 minutes.
3. Add beef chunks, butternut squash, and bell peppers.
4. Sauté until meat is no longer pink and vegetables have softened.
5. Press Keep Warm/Cancel button to end Sauté mode.
6. Add melted ghee, tomatoes, thyme, rosemary, parsley, cayenne pepper, salt and pepper. Stir well.
7. Close and seal lid. Press Manual button. Cook at High Pressure for 20 minutes.
8. Quick-release the pressure when done.. Open the lid with care. Stir ingredients. Adjust the seasoning if needed.
9. Serve.

Nutritional Information per serving:

Calories: 250, Fat: 7, Dietary Fiber: 2, Carbohydrates: 4g, Protein: 10g

29. Gratifying Meatloaf

Time: 35 minutes

Servings: 4

Ingredients:

- 3 pounds lean ground beef
- 4 garlic cloves, minced
- 1 yellow onion, chopped
- 1 cup mushrooms, chopped
- 3 large eggs
- ½ cup almond flour
- ¼ cup parmesan cheese, grated
- ¼ cup mozzarella cheese, grated
- ¼ cup fresh parsley, chopped
- 2 Tablespoons sugar-free ketchup
- 2 Tablespoons coconut oil
- 2 teaspoons salt
- 2 teaspoons black pepper
- 2 cups of water

Instructions:

1. Cover trivet with aluminum foil.
2. In a large bowl, add and mix all the ingredients (excluding the water) until well combined. Form into a meatloaf.
3. Pour the water in your Instant Pot. Place trivet inside.
4. Place meatloaf on trivet.
5. Close and seal lid. Press Manual button. Cook at High-Pressure for 25 minutes.
6. Release pressure naturally when done.. Open the lid with care.
7. Let the meatloaf rest for 5 minutes before slicing and serve.

Nutritional Information per serving:

Calories: 250, Fat: 15g, Dietary Fiber: 3g, Carbohydrates: 5g, Protein: 25g

30. Lavender Lamb Chops

Time: 25 minutes

Servings: 2

Ingredients:

- 2 lamb chops, boneless
- 2 Tablespoons ghee, melted
- 1 Tablespoon lavender, chopped
- 2 Tablespoons coconut oil
- 2 Tablespoons fresh rosemary, chopped
- Zest and juice from 1 orange
- Zest and juice from 1 lime
- 1 teaspoon garlic powder
- 1 teaspoon salt
- 1 teaspoon fresh ground black pepper
- 2 cups of water

Instructions:

1. Cover trivet with aluminum foil.
2. Press Sauté button on Instant Pot. Heat the coconut oil.
3. Sear lamb chops for 2 minutes per side. Remove and set aside.
4. Press Keep Warm/Cancel button to end Sauté mode.
5. In a bowl, add and mix the ghee, lavender, rosemary, orange juice, orange zest, lime juice, lime zest, and seasonings.
6. Pour 2 cups of water in Instant Pot. Place trivet inside. Set lamb chops on top.
7. Close and seal lid. Press Manual button. Cook at High Pressure for 15 minutes.
8. Quick-release the pressure when done. Open the lid with care.
9. Serve.

Nutritional Information per serving:

Calories: 250, Protein: 8g, Fat: 5g, Dietary Fiber: 1g, Carbohydrates: 5g

31. Lovely Ginger Beef and Kale

Time: 35 minutes

Servings: 4

Ingredients:

- 1 pound beef, cut into chunks
- 1 bunch of kale, stemmed and chopped
- ½ pound mushrooms, sliced
- 2 cups beef broth
- 1 red onion, chopped
- 4 garlic cloves, minced
- 2 Tablespoons fresh ginger, grated
- 2 Tablespoons coconut oil
- 1 teaspoon paprika
- 1 teaspoon salt
- 1 teaspoon fresh ground black pepper

Instructions:

1. Press Sauté button on Instant Pot. Heat the coconut oil.
2. Add onions and garlic. Sweat for 1 minute.
3. Add beef chunks. Sauté until meat is no longer pink.
4. Press Keep Warm/Cancel setting to end Sauté mode.
5. Add remaining ingredients. Stir well.
6. Close and seal lid. Press Manual button. Cook at High Pressure for 25 minutes.
7. When the timer beeps, quick-release or naturally release pressure. Open the lid with care. Stir ingredients. Adjust seasoning if necessary.
8. Serve.

Nutritional Information per serving:

Calories: 325, Fat: 15g, Carbohydrates: 20g, Dietary Fiber: 2.5g, Protein: 30g

32. Extraordinary Pork Roast

Time: 40 minutes

Servings: 4

Ingredients:

- 2 pounds pork roast
- 1 head cauliflower, chopped into florets
- 1 pound mushrooms, thinly sliced
- 2 Tablespoons coconut oil
- 1 onion, chopped
- 4 garlic cloves, minced
- 2 celery stalks, chopped
- 1 teaspoon salt
- 1 teaspoon fresh ground black pepper
- 2 cups beef broth

Instructions:

1. Press Sauté button on Instant Pot. Heat the coconut oil.
2. Sauté onion and garlic for 1 minute.
3. Season pork roast with salt and pepper. Sear on all sides.
4. Add cauliflower, mushrooms, and celery. Pour in beef broth. Stir.
5. Close and seal lid. Press Manual button. Cook at High Pressure for 30 minutes.
6. Release pressure naturally when done.. Open the lid with care. Stir ingredients.
7. Remove from Instant Pot. Let it sit for 5 – 10 minutes before slicing.
8. Serve.

Nutritional Information per serving:

Calories: 275, Carbohydrates: 10g, Fat: 10g, Dietary Fiber: 3g, Protein: 30g

33. Remarkable Apple Cider Pork Loin

Time: 40 minutes

Servings: 4

Ingredients:

- 4 pound pork loin
- 2 Tablespoons coconut oil
- 1 onion, sliced
- 4 garlic cloves, minced
- 1 cup apple cider
- 1 teaspoon salt
- 1 teaspoon fresh ground black pepper

Instructions:

1. Press Sauté mode on Instant Pot. Heat the coconut oil.
2. Season pork loin with salt and pepper. Sear all sides.
3. Press Keep Warm/Cancel button to end Sauté mode.
4. Pour in apple cider.
5. Close and seal lid. Press Manual button. Cook at High Pressure 30 minutes.
6. Quick-Release the pressure once done. Open the lid with care.
7. Let the roast rest for 5 – 10 minutes before slicing.
8. Serve.

Nutritional Information per serving:

Calories: 175, Fat: 10g, Carbohydrates: 0.5g, Protein: 21g, Dietary Fiber: 1g

34. Awe-Inspiring Lamb Roast

Time: 40 minutes

Servings: 4

Ingredients:

- 5 pound boneless leg of lamb, chopped
- 2 cups beef or vegetable broth
- 2 Tablespoons coconut oil
- 1 broccoli head, chopped into florets
- 1 onion, chopped
- 4 garlic cloves, minced
- 1 Tablespoon balsamic vinegar
- 1 teaspoon salt
- 1 teaspoon fresh ground black pepper
- 1 teaspoon fresh ginger, grated
- 1 teaspoon fresh thyme, chopped
- 1 Tablespoon fresh rosemary, chopped

Instructions:

1. Press Sauté button on Instant Pot. Heat the coconut oil.
2. Add the onion, garlic, ginger, thyme, rosemary. Sweat for 1 minute.
3. Season lamb with salt and pepper. Sear on all sides.
4. Press Keep Warm/Cancel button to end Sauté mode.
5. Add balsamic vinegar and beef broth. Stir well.
6. Close and seal cover. Press Manual switch. Cook at High Pressure for 30 minutes.
7. Quick-Release the pressure when done. Open the lid with care.
8. Let the roast rest for 5 – 10 minutes before slicing.
9. Serve.

Nutritional Information per serving:

Calories: 325, Fat: 15g, Protein: 20g, Carbohydrates: 6g, Dietary Fiber: 0.1g

35. Melt-in-Your-Mouth Salisbury Steak

Time: 35 minutes

Servings: 4

Steak Ingredients:

- 2 pounds lean ground beef
- 1 Tablespoon coconut oil
- ½ yellow onion, diced
- 2 garlic cloves, minced
- 1 Tablespoon bread crumbs
- 1 egg
- ¼ cup coconut flour
- ¼ cup beef broth
- 1 Tablespoon Worcestershire sauce
- 1 Tablespoon fresh parsley, chopped
- 1 teaspoon salt
- 1 teaspoon fresh ground black pepper

Gravy Ingredients:

- 2 Tablespoons ghee, melted
- 2 cups mushrooms, sliced
- 1 onion, sliced
- ½ cup beef broth
- ¼ cup sour cream
- 2 Tablespoons fresh parsley, chopped
- 1 Tablespoon tomato paste
- 1 teaspoon Worcestershire sauce
- 1 teaspoon salt
- 1 teaspoon fresh ground black pepper

Instructions:

1. In a large bowl, mix steak ingredients, except coconut oil.
2. Shape into round patties, ¼ inch thick. Set aside.
3. Press Sauté button on Instant Pot. Heat the coconut oil.
4. Cook patties 2 minutes per side, until golden brown.
5. Remove patties. Set aside.
6. Heat the ghee. Add gravy ingredients. Stir well.
7. Press Keep Warm/Cancel button to end Sauté mode.
8. Return patties to Instant Pot.
9. Close and seal cover. Press Manual switch. Cook at High Pressure for 25 minutes.
10. Quick-Release the pressure when done. Open the lid with care. Serve.

Nutritional Information per serving:

Calories: 425, Fat: 35g, Carbohydrates: 5g, Protein: 32g, Dietary Fiber: 1g

Chapter 4: Mouthwatering Seafood and Chicken

36. Spicy Spirited Lemon Salmon

Time: 20 minutes

Servings: 4

Ingredients:

- 4 salmon fillets
- Juice from 2 lemons + slices for garnish
- 1 cup of water
- 1 Tablespoon paprika
- 1 teaspoon cayenne pepper
- 1 teaspoon salt (to taste)
- 1 teaspoon fresh ground black pepper (to taste)

Instructions:

1. Rinse the salmon, pat dry.
2. In a bowl, combine salt, pepper, paprika, cayenne pepper.
3. Drizzle lemon juice over salmon fillet. Season with spice mixture. Turn over fillet, repeat on other side.
4. Add 1 cup of water to Instant Pot. Place trivet inside. Place fillets on trivet.
5. Close and seal cover. Press Manual button. Cook at High Pressure for 10 minutes.
6. Quick-Release the pressure when done. Open the lid with care.
7. Serve.

Nutritional Information per serving:

Calories: 280, Fat: 20g, Carbohydrates: 8g, Dietary Fiber: 0.5g, Protein 20.5g

37. Awesome Coconut Shrimp Curry

Time: 35 minutes

Servings: 4

Ingredients:

- 1 pound shrimp, peeled and deveined
- 1 Tablespoon coconut oil
- 4 garlic cloves, minced
- Juice from 1 lime
- 1 teaspoon salt
- 1 teaspoon fresh ground black pepper
- 4 tomatoes, chopped
- 1 red bell pepper, sliced
- 10-ounces coconut milk
- ½ cup fresh cilantro, chopped

Instructions:

1. Press Sauté mode on Instant Pot. Heat the coconut oil.
2. Season shrimp with lime juice, salt and pepper.
3. Sauté garlic for 1 minute.
4. Add shrimp. Cook 2 – 4 minutes per side.
5. Add bell peppers and tomatoes. Stir well.
6. Press Keep Warm/Cancel button to cancel Sauté mode.
7. Add coconut milk. Stir well.
8. Close and seal lid. Press Manual setting. Cook at High Pressure for 25 minutes.
9. Quick-Release the pressure when done. Open the lid with care.
10. Garnish with fresh cilantro. Serve.

Nutritional Information per serving:

Calories: 150, Fat: 3g, Dietary Fiber: 3g, Carbohydrates: 1g, Protein: 7g

38. Wondrous Mediterranean Fish

Time: 25 minutes

Servings: 4

Ingredients:

- 4 fish fillets (any kind)
- 1 pound cherry tomatoes, halved
- 1 cup green olives, pitted
- 2 garlic cloves, minced
- 1 cup of water
- 1 teaspoon coconut oil
- 1 Tablespoon fresh thyme, chopped
- 1 teaspoon fresh parsley
- 1 teaspoon salt (to taste)
- 1 teaspoon fresh ground black pepper (to taste)

Instructions:

1. Pour 1 cup of water in Instant Pot. Cover trivet in foil.
2. On a flat surface, rub fish fillets with garlic. Season with salt, pepper and thyme.
3. Place olives and cherry tomatoes along bottom of Instant Pot.
4. Place fillets on trivet.
5. Close and seal lid. Press Manual button. Cook at High Pressure for 15 minutes.
6. Release pressure naturally when done. Open the lid with care.
7. Place the fish with the ingredients. Stir to coat them.
8. Plate the fillets. Top with fresh parsley.
9. Serve.

Nutritional Information per serving:

Calories: 225, Fat: 4g, Protein: 30g, Dietary Fiber: 2.5g, Carbohydrates: 10g

39. Wild Alaskan Cod

Time: 25 minutes

Servings: 4

Ingredients:

- 4 wild Alaskan cod fillets
- 4 cups cherry tomatoes, halved
- 4 garlic cloves, minced
- 4 Tablespoons butter, melted
- 1 Tablespoon coconut oil
- ¼ cup of fresh cilantro, chopped
- 1 teaspoon salt (to taste)
- 1 teaspoon fresh ground black pepper (to taste)

Instructions:

1. On a flat surface, rub garlic over cod fillets. Season with salt and pepper.
2. Cover trivet with foil.
3. Add 1 cup of water to Instant Pot. Place trivet inside.
4. Place tomatoes along bottom of Instant Pot. Season with salt and pepper.
5. Place salmon fillets on trivet.
6. Pour melted butter and coconut oil over cod fillets and tomatoes.
7. Close and seal lid. Press Manual switch. Cook at High Pressure for 15 minutes.
8. When the timer beeps, quick-release pressure. Open the lid with care.
9. Plate the fillets. Top with tomatoes and fresh cilantro.
10. Serve.

Nutritional Information per serving:

Calories: 125, Fat: 5g, Carbohydrates: 0.5g, Protein: 25g, Dietary Fiber: 0g

40. Stunning Shrimp and Sausage Gumbo

Time: 35 minutes

Servings: 4

Ingredients:

- 1 pound shrimp, peeled and deveined
- 1 pound lean sausage, thinly sliced
- 1 red bell pepper, chopped
- 1 yellow onion, chopped
- 1 garlic clove, minced
- 1 celery stalk, chopped
- 2 cups chicken broth
- ½ cup fresh parsley, chopped
- 2 Tablespoons coconut oil
- 2 Tablespoons Cajun seasoning
- 1 teaspoon salt (to taste)
- 1 teaspoon fresh ground black pepper (to taste)

Instructions:

1. Press Sauté button on Instant Pot. Heat the coconut oil.
2. Sauté onion and garlic for 1 minute.
3. Add sausage and shrimp. Cook until golden brown.
4. Add bell pepper and celery. Season with Cajun spice. Stir well.
5. Press Keep Warm/Cancel setting to stop Sauté mode.
6. Add 2 cups of chicken broth. Stir well.
7. Close and seal lid. Press Meat/Stew button. Adjust to cook for 25 minutes.
8. When the timer beeps, quick-release or naturally release pressure. Open the lid with care. Stir well.
9. Serve.

Nutritional Information per serving:

Calories: 225, Fat: 15g, Carbohydrates: 5g, Protein: 30g, Dietary Fiber: 2.6g

41. Appetizing Steamed Crab Legs

Time: 20 minutes

Servings: 4

Ingredients:

- 2 pounds frozen crab legs
- 2 cups of water
- 4 Tablespoons butter, melted
- Juice from 1 lemon
- 1 teaspoon salt (to taste)
- 1 teaspoon fresh ground black pepper (to taste)

Instructions:

1. In a small bowl, combine melted butter, lemon juice, salt and pepper.
2. Add 2 cups of water to Instant Pot. Cover trivet in foil.
3. Place trivet in Instant Pot.
4. Place crab legs in single layer on trivet. Pour half butter mixture over crab.
5. Close and seal lid. Press Manual button. Cook at High Pressure for 10 minutes.
6. Quick-release the pressure when done. Open the lid with care.
7. Plate the crab legs. Pour remaining butter mixture over crab.
8. Serve.

Nutritional Information per serving:

Calories: 95, Carbohydrates: 0g, Dietary Fiber: 0g, Protein: 20g, Fat: 1g

42. Mouthwatering Parmesan Cod

Time: 30 minutes

Servings: 4

Ingredients:

- 4 cod fillets
- 4 green onions, minced
- 4 garlic cloves, minced
- ½ cup of parmesan cheese, grated
- 1 cup low-carb mayonnaise
- 1 teaspoon Worcestershire sauce
- 2 cups of water
- 1 teaspoon salt (to taste)
- 1 teaspoon fresh ground black pepper (to taste)

Instructions:

1. Add 2 cups of water in Instant Pot. Cover trivet with foil.
2. In a bowl, add green onions, garlic cloves, parmesan cheese, mayonnaise, Worcestershire sauce, salt, and black pepper. Stir well.
3. Coat cod fillets with mixture. Place on trivet.
4. Close and seal lid. Press Manual button. Cook at High Pressure for 20 minutes.
5. Quick-Release the pressure when done. Open the lid with care.
6. Let the cod rest for 5 minutes before removing.
7. Serve.

43. Lovely Tilapia Fillets

Time: 25 minutes

Servings: 4

Ingredients:

- 4 boneless, tilapia fillets
- ½ cup parmesan cheese, grated
- 4 Tablespoons low-carb mayonnaise
- ¼ cup ghee, melted
- 2 cups of water
- 1 teaspoon fresh basil, chopped
- 1 teaspoon onion powder
- Juice from ½ lemon
- 1 teaspoon garlic powder
- 1 teaspoon salt (to taste)
- 1 teaspoon fresh ground black pepper (to taste)

Instructions:

1. Pour 2 cups of water in Instant Pot. Cover trivet with foil.
2. In a bowl, combine parmesan cheese, mayonnaise, ghee, basil, lemon juice, and seasonings.
3. Coat tilapia fillets with mixture. Place the tilapia fillets on trivet.
4. Close and seal lid. Press Manual button. Cook at High Pressure for 15 minutes.
5. Quick-Release the pressure when done. Open the lid with care.
6. Allow the fish to rest for 5 minutes before removing.
7. Serve.

Nutritional Information per serving:

Calories: 175, Fat: 10g, Dietary Fiber: 0g, Carbohydrates: 5g, Protein: 17g

44. Generous Orange Trout Fillets

Time: 25 minutes

Servings: 4

Ingredients:

- 4 trout fillets
- 4 garlic cloves
- Zest and juice from 1 orange
- ¼ cup fresh parsley, chopped
- 1 cup pecans, roasted and chopped
- 1 Tablespoon ghee
- 2 cups of water
- 1 Tablespoon coconut oil
- 1 teaspoon salt (to taste)
- 1 teaspoon fresh ground black pepper (to taste)

Instructions:

1. Pour 2 cups of water in Instant Pot. Cover trivet with foil.
2. Combine orange juice and zest, garlic, parsley, ghee, coconut oil, salt, and pepper in a bowl. Stir well.
3. Cover trout with mixture. Place trout fillets on trivet.
4. Close and seal lid. Press Manual button. Cook at High Pressure for 15 minutes.
5. Quick-Release the pressure when done. Open the lid with care.
6. Plate the fillets. Serve.

Nutritional Information per serving:

Calories: 200, Fat: 10g, Dietary Fiber, 2g, Carbohydrates: 1g, Protein 11g

45. Intriguing Oysters

Time: 30 minutes

Servings: 4

Ingredients:

- 1 pound oysters, shucked
- 4 garlic cloves, minced
- ¼ cup fresh parsley, chopped
- 1 teaspoon paprika
- Juice from 1 lemon + slices for garnish
- 2 Tablespoons ghee, melted
- 2 cups of water
- 1 teaspoon salt (to taste)
- 1 teaspoon fresh ground black pepper (to taste)

Instructions:

1. Rinse the oysters.
2. In a bowl, combine garlic, parsley, paprika, lemon juice, ghee, salt, and black pepper.
3. Place the oysters in Instant Pot. Pour mixture over the oysters.
4. Close and seal the lid. Press Manual setting. Cook at High Pressure 20 minutes.
5. Quick-Release the pressure when done. Open the lid with care.
6. Serve. Top with lemon wedges.

Nutritional Information per serving:

Calories: 60, Fat: 1g, Dietary Fiber: 0, Carbohydrates: 0.5g, Protein: 1g

46. Robust Halibut Fillets

Time: 30 minutes

Servings: 4

Ingredients:

- 4 halibut fillets
- 6 garlic cloves, minced
- 4 green onions, chopped
- ¼ cup low-carb mayonnaise
- ¼ cup ghee, melted
- ¼ cup fresh parmesan cheese, grated
- ¼ cup mozzarella cheese, grated
- 1 teaspoon salt (to taste)
- 1 teaspoon fresh ground black pepper (to taste)
- Zest and juice from 1 lime
- 2 cups of water
- 1 lemon sliced for garnish
- Fresh parsley for garnish

Instructions:

1. Pour 2 cups of water in Instant Pot. Cover trivet with foil.
2. In a large mixing bowl, add the garlic, green onions, mayonnaise, ghee, cheeses, lime juice, lime zest, salt, and pepper. Stir well.
3. Coat the halibut fillets with the mixture. Place halibut on trivet.
4. Close and seal lid. Press Manual button. Cook at High Pressure for 20 minutes.
5. Once done, quick-release or naturally release pressure. Open the lid with care.
6. Plate the halibut. Top with fresh parsley, lemon slices. Serve.

Nutritional Information per serving:

Calories: 250, Fat: 12g, Dietary Fiber: 1g, Carbohydrates: 5g, Protein: 25g

47. Fantastic Chili Lime Cod

Time: 30 minutes

Servings: 4

Ingredients:

- 4 cod fillets, shredded
- 1 can (14-oucne) diced tomatoes
- 4 garlic cloves, minced
- 1 celery stalk, chopped
- 1 yellow onion, chopped
- 1 Tablespoon rice wine vinegar
- ½ cup low-carb mayonnaise
- ¼ cup fresh parsley, chopped
- Zest and juice from 1 lime
- 1 cup vegetable stock
- 1 Tablespoon coconut oil
- 1 teaspoon paprika
- 1 teaspoon salt
- 1 teaspoon fresh ground black pepper

Instructions:

1. Press Sauté mode on Instant Pot. Heat the coconut oil.
2. Add onion and garlic. Sauté for 1 minute. Add the celery and shredded cod.
3. Press Keep Warm/Cancel setting to stop Sauté mode.
4. Add diced tomatoes, mayonnaise, rice wine vinegar, parsley, lime juice, lime zest, and seasoning. Stir well.
5. Close and seal lid. Press Manual switch. Cook at High Pressure for 20 minutes.
6. Once done, quickly or naturally release pressure. Open the lid with care. Stir. Serve.

Nutritional Information per serving:

Calories: 215, Fat: 5g, Protein: 35g, Carbohydrates: 3g, Dietary Fiber: 2g

48. Delicious Cauliflower Risotto and Salmon

Time: 30 minutes

Servings: 4

Ingredients:

- 4 salmon fillets, shredded
- 1 pound asparagus, stemmed and chopped
- 1 head cauliflower, chopped into florets
- 8-ounce coconut cream, unsweetened
- 1 Tablespoon fresh or dried rosemary, chopped
- 2 teaspoons fresh or dried thyme, chopped
- ½ cup parmesan cheese, shredded
- 1 cup chicken broth
- 1 Tablespoon coconut oil
- 2 teaspoons salt (to taste)
- 1 teaspoon fresh ground black pepper (to taste)

Instructions:

1. In a food processor, add cauliflower florets. Pulse until rice-like consistency. Remove and set aside.
2. Press Sauté button on Instant Pot. Add the coconut oil, cauliflower rice, asparagus, and shredded salmon fillet. Cook until light brown and tender.
3. Press the Keep Warm/Cancel setting to stop the Sauté mode.
4. Add remaining ingredients. Stir well.
5. Close and seal lid. Press Manual button. Cook at High Pressure for 20 minutes.
6. Once done, naturally or quick-release pressure. Open the lid with care. Stir well.
7. Serve.

Nutritional Information per serving:

Calories: 225, Protein: 6g, Carbohydrates: 9, Fat: 20 g, Dietary Fiber: 3g

49. Tender Ginger Sesame Glaze Salmon

Time: 25 minutes

Servings: 4

Ingredients:

- 4 salmon fillets
- 4 garlic cloves, minced
- 1 Tablespoon fish sauce
- 1 Tablespoon fresh ginger, grated
- 1 Tablespoon sugar-free ketchup
- 2 Tablespoons white wine
- 1 Tablespoon rice vinegar
- 2 Tablespoons soy sauce
- 2 teaspoons sesame oil
- 2 cups of water

Instructions:

1. In a bowl, combine garlic, fish sauce, ginger, ketchup, white wine, rice vinegar, soy sauce, and sesame oil.
2. In a large Ziploc bag, add the sauce and salmon fillets. Marinate for 6 – 10 hours.
3. Pour 2 cups of water in Instant Pot. Cover trivet in foil. Place trivet in Instant Pot.
4. Place marinated salmon fillet on trivet.
5. Close and seal lid. Press Manual button. Cook at High Pressure for 15 minutes.
6. Once done, naturally release pressure. Open the lid with care.
7. Serve.

Nutritional Information per serving:

Calories: 370, Fat: 23.5g, Carbohydrates: 2.6g, Dietary Fiber: 0g, Protein: 33g

50. Supreme Chicken Breasts

Time: 20 minutes

Servings: 4

Ingredients:

- 4 chicken breasts, boneless, skinless
- 2 Tablespoons coconut oil
- 1 teaspoon salt (to taste)
- 1 teaspoon fresh ground black pepper (to taste)
- 2 cups of water

Instructions:

1. Cover trivet with foil.
2. Press Sauté button on Instant Pot. Heat the coconut oil.
3. Season the chicken with salt and pepper. Sauté for 2 minutes per side, until a golden crust forms. Remove chicken breasts and set aside.
4. Press Keep Warm/Cancel setting to end Sauté mode.
5. Pour 2 cups of water in the Instant Pot. Place trivet inside.
6. Place chicken breasts on trivet.
7. Close and seal lid. Press Manual button. Cook at High Pressure for 10 minutes.
8. When done, naturally release pressure. Open the lid with care. Let chicken rest for 5 minutes in Instant Pot.
9. Serve.

Nutritional Information per serving:

Calories: 100, Fat: 2g, Protein: 20g, Carbohydrates: 0g, Dietary Fiber: 0g

51. Delicious Cheesy Spinach Stuffed Chicken Breasts

Time: 20 minutes   Servings: 2

Ingredients:

- 2 chicken breasts
- 1 red bell pepper, chopped
- 1 cup mozzarella cheese, shredded
- 1 cup parmesan cheese, shredded
- 3 Tablespoons coconut oil
- 2 cups baby spinach
- 1 teaspoon garlic powder
- 1 teaspoon onion powder
- 1 teaspoon salt (to taste)
- 1 teaspoon fresh ground black pepper (to taste)
- 2 cups of water

Instructions:

1. Cover trivet with foil.
2. Press Sauté button on Instant Pot. Heat 2 tablespoons of the coconut oil.
3. Sauté the chicken until golden brown on both sides.
4. Remove the chicken breasts and allow to cool.
5. Press Keep Warm/Cancel button to end Sauté mode.
6. In a large bowl, combine red pepper, parmesan cheese, mozzarella cheese, 1 tablespoon of coconut oil, baby spinach, and seasoning.
7. When chicken is cool, cut down middle, but don't cut all the way through.
8. Stuff with the spinach mixture.
9. Pour 2 cups of water in Instant Pot. Place trivet inside. Place chicken on trivet.
10. Close and seal lid. Press Manual button. Cook at High Pressure for 7 minutes.
11. When done, naturally release pressure. Open the lid with care.
12. Allow chicken to rest 5 minutes.
13. Plate and serve.

Nutritional Information per serving:

Calories: 500, Fat: 33g, Carbohydrates: 3.7g, Protein: 45g, Dietary fiber: 1.7g

52. Royal Lemon Pepper Chicken

Time: 25 minutes

Servings: 4

Ingredients:

- 4 chicken breasts, skinless, boneless
- 2 Tablespoons coconut oil
- 2 Tablespoons butter, melted
- Zest and juice from 2 lemons
- 2 teaspoons salt (to taste)
- 1 Tablespoon lemon pepper seasoning (to taste)
- 2 Tablespoons fresh parsley, chopped

Instructions:

1. Press Sauté button on Instant Pot. Heat the coconut oil.
2. Sauté the chicken. Cook until golden brown on each side.
3. Press Keep Warm/Cancel setting to end Sauté mode.
4. In a bowl, add melted butter, lemon juice, lemon zest, salt, lemon pepper seasoning, and parsley. Stir well.
5. Coat chicken with seasoning mixture. Return chicken to Instant Pot.
6. Close and seal lid. Press Manual button. Cook at High Pressure for 5 minutes.
7. When done, naturally release pressure. Open the lid with care.
8. Allow chicken to rest for 5 minutes.
9. Serve.

Nutritional Information per serving:

Calories: 336, Fat: 25g, Carbohydrates: 5g, Dietary Fiber: 2g, Protein: 4g

53. Flaming Buffalo Chicken Strips

Time: 20 minutes

Servings: 2

Ingredients:

- 2 chicken breasts, boneless, skinless
- 1 cup of water
- 1 Tablespoon low-carb barbecue sauce
- 1 Tablespoon cayenne pepper
- 1 Tablespoon dried oregano
- 1 teaspoon garlic powder
- 1 teaspoon ground cumin
- 1 teaspoon chili powder
- 1 Tablespoon coconut oil
- 1 teaspoon salt (to taste)
- 1 teaspoon fresh ground black pepper (to taste)

Instructions:

1. Cover trivet in foil.
2. Press Sauté button on Instant Pot. Heat the coconut oil.
3. Add the chicken. Cook until brown on each side.
4. Remove the chicken breasts and set aside.
5. Press Keep Warm/Cancel setting to end Sauté mode.
6. Flavor the chicken with barbecue sauce, spices, and seasonings.
7. Pour water in Instant Pot. Place trivet in pot. Place chicken on trivet.
8. Close and seal lid. Press Manual button. Cook at High Pressure for 8 minutes.
9. When done, naturally release pressure. Open the lid with care.
10. Allow chicken to rest for 5 minutes. Serve.

Nutritional Information per serving:

Calories: 200, Fat: 9g, Carbohydrates: 20g, Dietary Fiber: 1g, Protein: 15g

54. Succulent Garlic Paprika Chicken Legs with Green Beans

Time: 20 minutes

Servings: 4

Ingredients:

- 4 chicken drumsticks
- 1 pound green beans, trimmed and chopped
- 1 cup chicken broth
- 1 Tablespoon coconut oil
- 2 Tablespoons onion powder
- 4 Tablespoons fresh herbs, chopped (rosemary, oregano, thyme)
- 1 Tablespoon smoked paprika
- 1 teaspoon salt
- 1 teaspoon fresh ground black pepper

Instructions:

1. In a bowl, combine fresh herbs and seasonings. Stir well.
2. In a large Ziploc bag, add chicken drumsticks and seasoning mixture.
3. Allow to marinate in refrigerator for 6 hours or overnight.
4. When ready to cook. Press Sauté button on Instant Pot. Heat the coconut oil.
5. Add the drumsticks. Cook until a golden crust forms.
6. Press Keep Warm/Cancel setting to end Sauté mode.
7. Add green beans and chicken broth to Instant Pot.
8. Close and seal lid. Press Manual button. Cook at High Pressure for 10 minutes.
9. Quick-release or naturally release pressure when done. Open the lid with care.
10. Allow chicken to rest for 5 minutes before removing.
11. Serve.

Nutritional Information per serving:

Calories: 160, Fat: 12g, Carbohydrates: 2g, Protein: 15g, Dietary Fiber: 1g

55. Phenomenal Whole Rotisserie Chicken

Time: 30 minutes

Servings: 6

Ingredients:

- 1 whole chicken
- Zest and juice from 1 lemon
- 2 cups chicken broth
- 2 Tablespoons coconut oil
- 2 teaspoons salt
- 2 teaspoons fresh ground black pepper
- 2 teaspoons paprika
- 2 Tablespoons fresh herbs, chopped
- 4 garlic cloves, minced

Instructions:

1. Remove any parts included inside chicken cavity. Rinse and pat dry.
2. In a bowl, combine the seasoning and herbs.
3. Pour coconut oil over the chicken. Rub seasoning mixture into chicken skin.
4. Press Sauté button on Instant Pot.
5. Place chicken in Instant Pot. Sauté all sides for 5 minutes.
6. Press Keep Warm/Cancel setting to stop Sauté mode.
7. Add chicken broth.
8. Close and seal lid. Press Manual switch. Cook at High Pressure for 25 minutes.
9. When done, naturally release pressure. Open the lid with care.
10. Allow to rest for 5 minutes before removing.
11. Serve.

Nutritional Information per serving:

Calories: 180, Fat: 13g, Protein: 17g, Carbohydrates: 0g, Dietary Fiber: 0g

Chapter 5: Vegan and Vegetarian

56. Unbelievable Zucchini with Avocado Sauce

Time: 15 minutes

Servings: 4

Ingredients:

- 2 pounds of zucchini, chopped
- 2 avocados, chopped
- Juice from 1 lime
- 1 shallot, chopped
- 2 garlic cloves, minced
- 1 cup of water
- 2 Tablespoons coconut oil
- ¼ cup fresh basil, chopped
- 1 teaspoon salt (to taste)
- 1 teaspoon fresh ground black pepper (to taste)

Instructions:

1. Press Sauté mode on Instant Pot. Heat the coconut oil.
2. Sauté garlic and shallots for 1 minute.
3. Press Keep Warm/Cancel setting to stop Sauté mode.
4. Add zucchini, avocado, basil, salt, and black pepper. Stir well.
5. Add the water. Stir well.
6. Close and seal lid. Press Manual setting. Cook at High Pressure for 5 minutes.
7. Quick-release or naturally release pressure. Open the lid with care. Stir ingredients.
8. Allow to cool down or refrigerate overnight.

Nutritional Information per serving:

Calories: 70, Dietary Fiber: 5g, Protein: 26g, Carbohydrates: 16g, Fat: 5g

57. Awesome Vegan Patties

Time: 15 minutes   Servings: 2

Ingredients:

- 2 cups mushrooms, chopped
- 1 onion, chopped
- 2 garlic cloves, minced
- 1 cup vegetable broth
- 1 Tablespoon ghee, melted
- 2 Tablespoons fresh basil, chopped
- 1 Tablespoon fresh oregano, chopped
- 1 teaspoon salt
- 1 teaspoon fresh ground black pepper
- 1 teaspoon fresh ginger, grated
- 2 ketogenic hamburger buns (to serve)
- 1 cup mixed lettuce (topping)

Instructions:

1. Press Sauté button on Instant Pot. Cover trivet in foil.
2. Add melted ghee, garlic cloves, onion, mushrooms, and ginger. Sauté until vegetables become translucent.
3. Press Keep Warm/Cancel setting to stop Sauté mode.
4. Add vegetable stock, basil, oregano, salt, and black pepper. Stir well.
5. Close and seal lid. Press Manual switch. Cook at High Pressure for 6 minutes.
6. Quick-release pressure when the timer goes off,. Allow to cool.
7. Mash ingredients with a fork or masher until smooth when cooled off. Form into patties.
8. Pour 2 cups of water in Instant Pot. Place trivet inside. Place patties on trivet.
9. Close and seal lid. Press Manual button. Cook at High Pressure for 7 minutes.
10.   Serve.

Nutritional Information per serving:

Calories: 300, Fat: 55g, Carbohydrates: 8g, Dietary Fiber: 10g, Protein: 23g

58. Scrumptious Brussels Sprouts

Time: 15 minutes

Servings: 4

Ingredients:

- 1 pound Brussels sprouts
- 2 Tablespoons coconut oil
- 1 teaspoon salt
- 1 teaspoon fresh ground black pepper

Instructions:

1. Add 2 cups of water in Instant Pot. Place trivet in Instant Pot. Place steamer basket on top.
2. Add Brussels sprouts to steamer basket. Drizzle with coconut oil; sprinkle with salt and black pepper.
3. Close and seal lid. Press Manual switch. Cook at High Pressure for 7 minutes.
4. When done, quickly release pressure. Open the lid with care.
5. Serve.

Nutritional Information per serving:

Calories: 70, Protein: 8g, Dietary Fiber: 5g, Carbohydrates: 5g, Fat: 0.5g

59. Wonderful Eggplant Lasagna

Time: 30 minutes   Servings: 4

Ingredients:

- 1 pound of eggplant, sliced
- 4 garlic cloves, minced
- 2 Tablespoons coconut oil
- Juice from 1 lemon
- 1 cup vegetable broth
- 6 cups low-carb tomato sauce
- 1 cup mozzarella cheese, shredded
- 1 cup parmesan cheese, grated
- 1 cup ricotta cheese
- 1 Tablespoon fresh basil leaves, chopped
- 1 Tablespoon fresh oregano, chopped
- 1 Tablespoon paprika
- 1 teaspoon salt
- 1 teaspoon fresh ground black pepper

Instructions:

1. Grease a baking dish with non-stick cooking spray.
2. In a bowl, combine the cheeses and herbs.
3. In a separate bowl, add and season the eggplants with garlic cloves, lemon juice, paprika, salt, and black pepper.
4. Layer baking dish with eggplant slices, tomato sauce. Sprinkle mixed cheeses. Repeat.
5. Cover baking dish with aluminum foil.
6. Add 2 cups of water. Place trivet in Instant Pot. Place dish on trivet.
7. Close and seal lid. Press Manual switch. Cook at High Pressure for 25 minutes.
8. When done, naturally release or quickly release pressure. Open the lid with care.
9. Serve.

Nutritional Information per serving:

Calories: 240, Fat: 13g, Carbohydrates: 10g, Dietary Fiber: 5g, Protein: 20g

60. Won't Know it's Vegan Chili

Time: 35 minutes   Servings: 4

Ingredients:

- 1 eggplant, chopped
- 1 jalapeno, chopped
- 1 red bell pepper, chopped
- 1 green bell pepper, chopped
- 1 zucchini, chopped
- 4 garlic cloves, minced
- 1 onion, chopped
- ½ pound mushrooms, chopped
- 2 Tablespoons coconut oil
- 2 cups vegetable broth
- 1 can (6-ounce) tomato paste
- 1 can (14-oucne) diced tomatoes
- 1 Tablespoon Chili powder
- 1 teaspoon ground cumin
- 1 teaspoon salt (to taste)
- 1 teaspoon fresh ground black pepper (to taste)

Instructions:

1. Press Sauté button on Instant Pot. Heat the coconut oil.
2. Add eggplant, jalapeno, bell peppers, zucchinis, garlic cloves, onion, and mushrooms. Sauté until vegetables become soft.
3. Press Keep Warm/Cancel setting to stop Sauté mode.
4. Add tomato paste. Stir well.
5. Add vegetable broth, diced tomatoes, and seasonings. Stir well.
6. Close and seal lid. Press Bean/Chili button. Cook for 30 minutes.
7. Naturally release or quick-release pressure when complete.
8. Stir chili. Adjust seasoning if necessary. Serve.

Nutritional Information per serving:

Calories: 200, Fat: 6g, Carbohydrates: 5g, Protein: 15g, Dietary Fiber: 1g

61. Buddha's Tofu and Broccoli Delight

Time: 15 minutes

Servings: 4

Ingredients:

- 1 pound of tofu, extra firm, chopped into cubes
- 1 broccoli head, chopped into florets
- 1 onion, chopped
- 1 carrot, chopped
- 4 garlic cloves, minced
- 2 Tablespoons low-carb brown sugar
- 1 Tablespoon fresh ginger, grated
- 1 Tablespoon rice vinegar
- 1 cup vegetable broth
- 2 scallions, chopped
- 2 Tablespoons coconut oil
- 1 teaspoon salt (to taste)
- 1 teaspoon fresh ground black pepper (to taste)

Instructions:

1. Press Sauté button on Instant Pot. Heat the coconut oil.
2. Sauté garlic and onion for 2 minutes.
3. Add broccoli florets and tofu. Sauté for 3 minutes.
4. Press Keep Warm/Cancel button to end Sauté mode.
5. Add remaining ingredients. Stir well.
6. Close and seal lid. Press Manual setting. Cook at High Pressure for 6 minutes.
7. When the timer beeps, quick-release pressure. Open the lid with care.
8. Serve.

Nutritional Information per serving:

Calories: 330, Fat: 25g, Carbohydrates: 10g, Protein: 25g, Dietary Fiber: 3g

62. Special Spicy Almond Tofu

Time: 25 minutes

Servings: 4

Ingredients:

- 1 pound extra firm tofu, chopped into cubes
- 1 cauliflower head, chopped into florets
- 1 broccoli head, chopped into florets
- 1 cup almonds, roughly chopped
- 2 Tablespoons low-carb soy sauce
- 2 Tablespoons green Chili Sauce
- 2 Tablespoons coconut oil
- 1 teaspoon garlic powder
- 1 teaspoon onion powder
- 1 teaspoon salt (to taste)
- 1 teaspoon fresh ground black pepper (to taste)

Instructions:

1. Press Sauté button on Instant Pot. Heat the coconut oil.
2. Add tofu, cauliflower florets, and broccoli florets. Sauté until fork tender.
3. Press Keep Warm/Cancel setting to end Sauté mode.
4. Add remaining ingredients to Instant Pot. Stir well.
5. Close and seal lid. Press Manual switch. Cook at High Pressure for 10 minutes.
6. When the timer beeps, naturally release or quickly release pressure. Open the lid with care. Stir ingredients.
7. Serve.

Nutritional Information per serving:

Calories: 155, Fat: 10g, Carbohydrates: 10g, Protein: 5g, Dietary Fiber: 0.9g

63. Fresh Garlic Cauliflower and Sweet Potato Mash

Time: 20 minutes

Servings: 4

Ingredients:

- 2 pounds sweet potatoes, chopped
- 1 head cauliflower, chopped into florets
- 4 garlic cloves, minced
- 2 Tablespoons coconut oil
- 1 teaspoon salt (to taste)
- 1 teaspoon fresh ground black pepper (to taste)
- 2 cups of water

Instructions:

1. Press Sauté button on Instant Pot. Heat the coconut oil.
2. Sauté sweet potatoes, cauliflower, and garlic. Sauté until almost tender.
3. Press Keep Warm/Cancel button to end Sauté mode.
4. Add the water to your ingredients.
5. Close and seal lid. Press Manual switch. Cook at High Pressure for 10 minutes.
6. When the timer beeps, quick-release pressure. Mash ingredients in Pot until smooth.
7. Serve.

Nutritional Information per serving:

Calories: 250, Fat: 0.5g, Carbohydrates: 20g, Protein: 10g, Dietary Fiber: 5g

64. Everyday Bold Beet and Caper Salad

Servings: 2

Time: 30 minutes

Ingredients:

- 4 beets, sliced
- 4 carrots, sliced
- 1 cup pine nuts, chopped
- 2 Tablespoons rice wine vinegar
- 1 cup of water

Dressing Ingredients:

- 1 Tablespoon coconut oil, melted and cooled
- ¼ cup fresh parsley, chopped
- 2 garlic cloves, minced
- 2 Tablespoons capers
- 4-ounces goat cheese, crumbled
- 1 teaspoon salt
- 1 teaspoon fresh ground black pepper

Instructions:

1. Pour 1 cup of water in Instant Pot.
2. Place a trivet inside; place steamer basket on top.
3. Add sliced beets, pine nuts, and carrots to steamer basket.
4. Drizzle with rice wine vinegar.
5. Close and seal lid. Press Manual setting. Cook at High Pressure for 20 minutes.
6. As it cooks, in a large bowl, combine dressing ingredients. Stir well. Set aside. When done, naturally release pressure. Open the lid with care.
7. In a large bowl, combine the beets and carrots with dressing. Stir until coated. Serve.

Nutritional Information per serving:

Calories: 90, Fat: 5g, Carbohydrates: 4g, Dietary Fiber: 1g, Protein: 2g

65. Fragrant Zucchini Mix

Servings: 4

Time: 15 minutes

Ingredients:

- 2 pounds zucchini, roughly chopped
- 1 broccoli head, chopped into florets
- 1 red onion, chopped
- 2 garlic cloves, minced
- 2 Tablespoons coconut oil
- 1 cup of water
- 2 cups fresh basil, chopped
- 1 teaspoon salt (to taste)
- 1 teaspoon fresh ground black pepper (to tastes)

Instructions:

1. Press Sauté button on Instant Pot. Heat the coconut oil.
2. Sauté onion and garlic for 1 minute.
3. Add broccoli florets and zucchini. Sauté until the vegetables become soft.
4. Press Keep Warm/Cancel setting to end Sauté mode.
5. Add remaining ingredients to vegetables. Stir well.
6. Close and seal lid. Press Manual switch. Cook at High Pressure for 7 minutes.
7. When the timer goes off, quick-release pressure. Open the lid with care.
8. Serve.

Nutritional Information per serving:

Calories: 70, Fat: 10g, Carbohydrates: 5g, Protein: 3g Dietary Fiber: 0.7g

66. Not Your Average Mushroom Risotto

Time: 15 minutes   Servings: 2

Ingredients:

- 2 pounds cremini mushrooms, chopped
- 1 pound extra firm tofu, chopped into cubes
- Bunch of baby spinach, freshly chopped
- 1 Tablespoon ghee
- 1 Tablespoon nutritional yeast
- 4 garlic cloves, minced
- ⅓ cup parmesan cheese, shredded
- 1 red onion, chopped
- 2 Tablespoons coconut oil
- ¼ cup dry white wine
- 3 cups vegetable broth
- Zest and juice from 1 lemon
- 1 teaspoon fresh thyme, chopped
- 1 teaspoon salt (to taste)
- 1 teaspoon fresh ground black pepper (to taste)

Instructions:

1. Press Sauté button on Instant Pot. Melt the ghee.
2. Sauté garlic and onion for 1 minute.
3. Add tofu and mushrooms. Cook until softened.
4. Press Keep Warm/Cancel button to end Sauté mode.
5. Add remaining ingredients. Stir well.
6. Close and seal lid. Press Manual setting. Cook at High Pressure for 8 minutes.
7. Quick-Release the pressure when done. Open the lid with care.
8. Press Sauté button. Cook until mixture thickens. Press Keep Warm/Cancel. Serve.

Nutritional Information per serving:

Calories: 300, Fat: 18g, Protein: 6g, Carbohydrates: 10g, Dietary Fiber: 3g

Chapter 6: Side Dishes, Stocks, and Sauces

67. Ultimate Corn on the Cob

Time: 15 minutes

Servings: 4

Ingredients:

- 8 corn on the cob
- 2 cups of water
- 2 teaspoons low-carb brown sugar
- 1 teaspoon salt (to taste)
- 1 teaspoon fresh ground black pepper (to taste)

Instructions:

1. Pour 2 cups of water in Instant Pot.
2. Place corn in steamer basket. Place basket in Instant Pot.
3. Close and seal lid. Press Manual button. Cook at High Pressure for 5 minutes.
4. When the timer beeps, naturally release pressure. Open the lid with care.
5. Sprinkle with brown sugar.
6. Serve.

Nutritional Information per serving:

Calories: 80, Fat: 1g, Carbohydrates: 25g, Fat: 3.5g, Dietary Fiber: 1g, Protein: 4.5g

68. Tangy Steamed Artichokes

Time: 25 minutes

Servings: 2

Ingredients:

- 2 artichokes
- Juice from 1 lemon
- 2 Tablespoons low-carb mayonnaise
- 2 cups of water
- 1 teaspoon paprika
- 1 teaspoon salt (to taste)
- 1 teaspoon fresh ground black pepper (to taste)

Instructions:

1. Wash and trim artichokes.
2. Pour 2 cups of water in Instant Pot.
3. Place artichokes in steamer basket. Place basket in Instant Pot.
4. Close and seal lid. Press Manual switch. Cook at High Pressure for 10 minutes.
5. Release pressure naturally when done. Open the lid with care.
6. In a bowl, combine mayonnaise, lemon juice, paprika, salt, and black pepper. Spread on artichokes.
7. Serve.

Nutritional Information per serving:

Calories: 80g, Protein: 3g, Carbohydrates: 0g, Fat: 5g, Protein: 4.2g

69. Succulent Sausage and Cheese Dip

Time: 10 minutes

Servings: 4

Ingredients:

- 1 pound ground Italian sausage
- ¼ cup green onions, chopped
- 1 cup cream cheese, softened
- 1 cup mozzarella cheese, shredded
- 1 cup cheddar cheese, shredded
- 1 cup vegetable broth
- 2 cups canned diced tomatoes
- 2 Tablespoons ghee, melted

Instructions:

1. Press Sauté button on Instant Pot. Heat the ghee.
2. Sauté Italian sausage and green onions, until sausage is brown.
3. Add remaining ingredients. Stir well.
4. Close and seal lid. Press Manual button. Cook at High Pressure for 5 minutes.
5. When the timer beeps, naturally release pressure. Open the lid with care.
6. Serve.

Nutritional Information per serving:

Calories: 155, Fat: 12, Dietary Fiber: 1g, Carbohydrates: 3g, Protein: 8g

70. Zesty Onion and Cauliflower Dip

Time: 20 minutes

Servings: 4

Ingredients:

- 1 head cauliflower, minced
- 1 cup chicken broth
- 1 ¼ cup low-carb mayonnaise
- 1 onion, chopped
- 1 cup cream cheese, softened
- 1 teaspoon Chili powder
- 1 teaspoon ground cumin
- 1 teaspoon garlic powder
- 1 teaspoon salt (to taste)
- 1 teaspoon fresh ground black pepper (to taste)

Instructions:

1. Add all ingredients to Instant Pot. Stir well.
2. Using a hand blender, blend ingredients.
3. Close and seal lid. Press Manual button. Cook at High Pressure for 10 minutes.
4. When the timer beeps, naturally release pressure, Open the lid with care. Stir ingredients.
5. Serve.

Nutritional Information per serving:

Calories: 86, Fat: 5g, Dietary Fiber: 1g, Carbohydrates: 1g, Protein: 1.6g

71. Ravishing Mushrooms and Sausage Gravy

Time: 15 minutes

Servings: 4

Ingredients:

- 1 pound Italian ground sausage
- 2 Tablespoons coconut oil
- 1 yellow onion, diced
- 2 garlic cloves, minced
- 2 cups mushrooms, chopped
- 1 red bell pepper, minced
- 2 Tablespoons ghee, melted
- ⅓ cup coconut flour
- 3½ cups coconut milk, unsweetened
- ½ cup organic heavy cream
- 1 teaspoon salt (to taste)
- 1 teaspoon fresh ground black pepper (to taste)

Instructions:

1. Press Sauté button on Instant Pot. Heat the coconut oil.
2. Sauté onion and garlic for 2 minutes.
3. Add the Italian sausage. Cook until brown.
4. Add mushrooms, bell peppers and sauté until soft. Season with salt and pepper. Press Keep Warm/Cancel button to end Sauté mode.
5. In a small saucepan, over medium heat, melt the ghee. Add the flour. Whisk in coconut milk and heavy cream. Continue stirring until thickens. Add flour mixture to Instant Pot. Stir well.
6. Close and seal lid. Press Manual button. Cook at High Pressure for 10 minutes. When the timer beeps, naturally release pressure. Open the lid with care. Serve.

Nutritional Information per serving:

Calories: 130, Fat: 12g, Protein: 3g, Dietary Fiber: 0.8g, Carbohydrates: 6g

72. Flawless Cranberry Sauce

Time: 20 minutes

Servings: 4

Ingredients:

- 12-ounces fresh cranberries
- ¼ cup red wine
- 1 Tablespoon granulated Splenda
- Juice from 1 orange
- ⅛ teaspoon salt

Instructions:

1. Add all ingredients to Instant Pot. Stir well.
2. Close and seal lid. Press Manual switch. Cook at High Pressure for 2 minutes.
3. When the timer beeps, naturally release pressure. Open the lid with care.
4. Crush the cranberries with a fork or masher. Stir again.
5. Serve warm or cold.

Nutritional Information per serving:

Calories: 50, Fat: 0g, Carbohydrates: 6g, Dietary Fiber: 2g, Protein: 0g

73. Perfect Marinara Sauce

Time: 15 minutes

Servings: 2

Ingredients:

- 2 (14-ounce) cans diced tomatoes
- 2 Tablespoons red wine vinegar
- ¼ cup coconut oil
- 1 teaspoon onion powder
- 1 teaspoon garlic powder
- 1 Tablespoon fresh oregano, chopped
- 1 Tablespoon fresh basil, chopped
- 1 Tablespoon fresh parsley, chopped
- 1 teaspoon salt
- 1 teaspoon fresh ground black pepper

Instructions:

1. Add the ingredients to Instant Pot. Stir well.
2. Close and seal lid. Press Manual button. Cook at High Pressure for 8 minutes.
3. When the timer beeps, naturally release pressure. Open the lid with care.
4. Puree mixture with immersion blender.
5. Serve.

Nutritional Information per serving:

Calories: 80, Fat: 7g, Carbohydrates: 3g, Protein: 1g, Dietary Fiber: 0g

74. Very Cheesy Cheese Sauce

Time: 10 minutes

Servings: 2

Ingredients:

- 2 Tablespoons ghee
- ½ cup cream cheese, softened
- 1 cup cheddar cheese, grated
- 1 cup mozzarella cheese, grated
- 2 Tablespoons water (or coconut milk)
- ½ cup heavy whipping cream
- 1 teaspoon of salt

Instructions:

1. Press Sauté button on Instant Pot. Melt the ghee.
2. Add cream cheese, cheddar cheese, mozzarella cheese, water or/coconut milk, heavy whipping cream, and salt. Stir constantly until melted.
3. Press Keep Warm/Cancel button to end sauté mode.
4. Close and seal lid. Press Manual switch. Cook at High Pressure for 4 minutes.
5. Quick-release or naturally release pressure when done. Open the lid with care. Stir.
6. Serve.

Nutritional Information per serving:

Calories: 200, Fat: 20g, Protein: 5g, Dietary Fiber: 0g, Carbohydrates: 1g

75. Best Homemade Alfredo Sauce

Time: 15 minutes

Servings: 2

Ingredients:

- 1 cup coconut milk
- 2 cups Parmesan cheese, grated
- 1 onion, chopped
- 1 teaspoon of salt
- ½ lemon, juice
- ¼ cup + 1 Tablespoon nutritional yeast
- 2 Tablespoons ghee
- 1 teaspoon garlic powder
- 1 teaspoon ground nutmeg
- 1 teaspoon salt
- 1 teaspoon fresh ground black pepper

Instructions:

1. Press Sauté button on Instant Pot. Heat the ghee.
2. Sauté the garlic and onion until become translucent.
3. Add coconut milk, parmesan cheese, nutritional yeast, lemon juice, and seasonings. Stir constantly until smooth.
4. Press Keep Warm/Cancel button. Cook at High Pressure for 6 minutes.
5. Quick-release or naturally release pressure when done. Open the lid with care. Stir.
6. Serve.

Nutritional Information per serving:

Calories: 200g, Fat: 31g, Dietary Fiber: 0.7g, Protein: 12g, Carbohydrates: 8g

76. Hot Dogs with a Twist

Time: 10 minutes

Servings: 4

Ingredients:

- 8 hot dogs
- 1 cup low-carb beer
- 8 ketogenic hot dog buns (for serving)

Instructions:

1. Place the hot dogs in Instant Pot.
2. Pour beer over the hot dogs.
3. Close and seal the lid. Press Manual button. Cook at High Pressure for 5 minutes.
4. Quick-Release the pressure when done. Open the lid with care.
5. Serve, on buns or alone.

Nutritional Information per serving:

Calories: 300, Fat: 20g, Carbohydrates: 5g, Protein: 10g, Dietary Fiber: 0.5g

77. Knockout Asparagus and Shrimp Mix

Time: 10 minutes

Servings: 4

Ingredients:

- 1 pound asparagus, trimmed and chopped
- 1 pound shrimp, peeled and deveined
- 2 Tablespoons ghee, melted
- 2 cups of water
- 1 teaspoon salt (to taste)
- 1 teaspoon fresh ground black pepper (to taste)

Instructions:

1. Pour 2 cups of water in Instant Pot.
2. Place shrimp and asparagus in steamer basket. Drizzle melted ghee over shrimp and asparagus. Season with salt and pepper. Place basket in Instant Pot.
3. Close and seal lid. Press Manual button. Cook at High Pressure for 6 minutes.
4. When the timer beeps, release pressure naturally. Open the lid with care.
5. Serve.

Nutritional Information per serving:

Calories: 150, Fat: 2g, Dietary Fiber: 4g, Carbohydrates: 10g, Protein: 24g

78. Heavenly Stuffed Bell Peppers

Time: 30 minutes

Servings: 4

Ingredients:

- 1 pound lean ground beef
- 1 teaspoon coconut oil
- 4 medium to large bell peppers, de-seeded, tops sliced off
- 1 avocado, chopped
- Juice from 1 lime
- 1 jalapeno, minced (depending on heat level, remove or leave seeds)
- 2 green onions, chopped
- 2 cups of water
- 1 cup mixed cheeses, shredded
- 2 teaspoons chili powder
- 1 teaspoon garlic powder
- 1 teaspoon ground cumin
- 1 teaspoon salt (to taste)
- 1 teaspoon fresh ground black pepper (to taste)

Instructions:

1. Press Sauté button on Instant Pot. Heat the coconut oil.
2. Sauté ground beef until no longer pink; drain.
3. Place ground beef in a bowl. Add green onions, jalapeno, and seasoning. Stir well.
4. Stuff mixture in bell peppers.
5. Pour 2 cups of water in Instant Pot. Place stuffed peppers in steamer basket. Top with shredded cheese.
6. Close and seal lid. Press Manual button. Cook at High Pressure for 15 minutes.
7. When done, naturally release pressure. Open the lid with care. Serve.

Nutritional Information per serving:

Calories: 200, Fat: 5g, Protein: 15g, Carbohydrates: 10g, Dietary Fiber: 3.3g

79. Delicious Broccoli and Garlic Combo

Time: 15 minutes

Servings: 4

Ingredients:

- 1 broccoli head, chopped into florets
- 2 Tablespoons coconut oil
- 6 garlic cloves, minced
- 2 cups of water
- 1 teaspoon salt (to taste)
- 1 teaspoon black pepper (to taste)

Instructions:

1. Press Sauté button on Instant Pot. Heat the coconut oil.
2. Sauté garlic for 2 minutes. Add the broccoli. Cook until softened. Set aside.
3. Press Keep Warm/Cancel button to end Sauté mode.
4. Pour 2 cups of water in Instant Pot. Place garlic and broccoli florets in steamer basket. Season with salt and black pepper.
5. Close and seal lid. Press Manual button. Cook at High Pressure for 10 minutes.
6. When done, naturally release pressure. Open the lid with care.
7. Transfer to a bowl. Stir well.
8. Serve.

Nutritional Information per serving:

Calories: 100, Fat: 1g, Dietary Fiber: 0g, Carbohydrates: 3g, Protein: 7g

80. Hollywood Collard Greens and Bacon

Time: 15 minutes

Servings: 4

Ingredients:

- 1 pound collard greens, trimmed and chopped
- ¼ pound bacon, chopped
- ½ cup ghee, melted
- 1 teaspoon salt
- 1 teaspoon fresh ground black pepper

Instructions:

1. Press Sauté button on Instant Pot. Melt 1 tablespoon of ghee.
2. Add the bacon. Sauté until bacon is brown and crispy.
3. Press Keep Warm/Cancel button to end Sauté mode.
4. Add collard greens, rest of the ghee, salt and pepper. Stir well.
5. Close and seal lid. Press Manual button. Cook at High Pressure for 10 minutes.
6. When done, naturally release pressure. Open the lid with care. Stir.
7. Serve.

Nutritional Information per serving:

Calories: 130, Fat: 8g, Dietary Fiber: 2g, Carbohydrates: 4g, Protein: 6g

81. Godly Kale Delish

Time: 15 minutes

Servings: 4

Ingredients:

- 1 bunch of kale, trimmed and chopped
- 1 red onion, thinly sliced
- 4 garlic cloves, minced
- 1 cup pine nuts, roughly chopped
- 1 cup vegetable broth
- 1 Tablespoon ghee, melted
- 2 Tablespoons coconut oil
- 1 Tablespoon balsamic vinegar
- 1 teaspoon red pepper flakes
- 1 teaspoon salt
- 1 teaspoon fresh ground black pepper

Instructions:

1. Press Sauté button on Instant Pot. Heat the coconut oil.
2. Sauté onion and garlic until translucent.
3. Press Keep Warm/Cancel button to end Sauté mode.
4. Add kale, pine nuts, melted ghee, balsamic vinegar, pine nuts, red pepper flakes, salt and pepper. Stir well.
5. Close and seal lid. Press Manual button. Cook at High Pressure for 8 minutes.
6. Quick-Release the pressure when done. Open the lid with care.
7. Adjust seasoning if needed.
8. Serve.

Nutritional Information per serving:

Calories: 75, Fat: 2g, Dietary Fiber: 2g, Carbohydrates: 4g, Protein: 1g

Chapter 7: Festival & Weekend Recipes

82. Authentic Indian Butter Chicken

Time: 25 minutes

Servings: 4

Ingredients:

- 4 chicken breasts, boneless, skinless
- 2 jalapeno peppers, chopped (remove seeds)
- 1 onion, chopped
- 4 garlic cloves, minced
- 1 cup heavy cream
- 2 teaspoons garam masala
- 1 cup Greek yogurt
- 2 Tablespoons cornstarch
- 2 Tablespoons chicken stock
- ¼ cup of fresh cilantro, chopped
- 2 (14-ounce) cans diced tomatoes
- 2 Tablespoons fresh ginger, grated
- ½ cup ghee, melted
- 2 Tablespoons coconut oil
- 2 teaspoons ground cumin
- 1 teaspoon cayenne pepper
- 1 teaspoon salt (to taste)
- 1 teaspoon fresh ground black pepper (to taste)

Instructions:

1. Rinse chicken, pat dry. Cut into chunks.
2. In a food processor, add canned tomatoes, ginger, jalapenos. Pulse until blended.
3. Press Sauté button on Instant Pot. Heat the coconut oil.
4. Sauté onion and garlic for 2 minutes, Add chicken breasts. Brown on all sides.
5. Press Keep Warm/Cancel button to stop Sauté mode.
6. Add rest of ingredients, including pureed tomato mixture. Stir well.
7. Close and seal lid. Press Manual button. Cook at High Pressure for 10 minutes.
8. When the timer beeps, quick-release pressure. Open the lid with care. Stir well.
9. Serve.

Nutritional Information per serving:

Calories: 350, Fat: 30g, Dietary Fiber: 2g, Carbohydrates: 8g, Protein: 24g

83. Rockstar Chicken Wings

Time: 20 minutes

Servings: 4

Ingredients:

- 1 pound chicken wings
- 6 garlic cloves, minced
- 1 Tablespoon fresh ginger, grated
- 2 Tablespoons coconut oil
- 1 Tablespoon fresh rosemary, chopped
- 1 Tablespoon fresh thyme, chopped
- 1 teaspoon salt
- 1 teaspoon fresh ground black pepper
- 2 cups chicken broth

Instructions:

1. Drizzle coconut oil over chicken wings, turning so they are coated.
2. Season with ginger, rosemary, thyme, salt, and black pepper.
3. Press Sauté button on Instant Pot.
4. Sauté chicken wings until golden brown. Add garlic while cooking.
5. Press Keep Warm/cancel setting to end Sauté mode.
6. Add chicken broth.
7. Close and seal lid. Press Manual button. Cook at High Pressure for 8 minutes.
8. When the timer beeps, naturally release pressure. Open the lid with care.
9. Serve.

Nutritional Information per serving:

Calories: 187, Fat: 10g, Dietary Fiber: 0g, Carbohydrates: 6g, Protein: 18g

84. Festive Okra Pilaf

Time: 25 minutes

Servings: 4

Ingredients:

- 1 pound okra, sliced
- 8 bacon slices, minced
- 2 cups cauliflower rice
- 1 cup tomatoes, minced
- 2 cups of water
- 1 Tablespoon ghee, melted
- 2 teaspoons paprika
- ¼ cup fresh cilantro, chopped
- 1 teaspoon salt
- 1 teaspoon fresh ground black pepper

Instructions:

1. Press Sauté button on Instant Pot.
2. Cook bacon until brown.
3. Sauté okra and cauliflower rice until softened.
4. Add remaining ingredients. Stir well.
5. Close and seal lid. Press Manual button. Cook at High Pressure for 10 minutes.
6. Quick-Release the pressure when done. Open the lid with care.
7. Serve.

Nutritional Information per serving:

Calories: 300, Fat: 12g, Dietary Fiber: 4g, Protein: 8g, Carbohydrates: 5g

Chapter 8: Special Occasion Recipes

85. Thankful Thanksgiving Whole Turkey

Time: 45 minutes

Servings: 6

Ingredients:

- 1 whole turkey (large enough for your Instant Pot)
- 1 Tablespoon fresh rosemary, chopped
- 1 Tablespoon fresh thyme, chopped
- 1 Tablespoon fresh sage, chopped
- 2 Tablespoons coconut oil
- 1 cup white wine vinegar
- 2 cups turkey or chicken broth
- 2 teaspoons onion powder
- 2 teaspoons garlic powder
- 2 teaspoons paprika
- 2 teaspoons salt
- 2 teaspoons fresh ground black pepper

Instructions:

1. Remove all parts in turkey cavity. Wash and pat dry.
2. Drizzle coconut oil over the turkey.
3. Combine seasoning and herbs. Rub all over surface of turkey.
4. Press Sauté button on Instant Pot.
5. Place turkey in Instant Pot. Sauté for 3 minutes; flip cook another 3 minutes. (Don't worry if parts of turkey are not golden brown.)
6. Press Keep Warm/Cancel setting to stop Sauté mode.
7. Pour white vinegar and broth over your turkey.
8. Close and seal lid. Press Manual switch. Cook at High Pressure for 30 minutes.
9. When the timer beeps, naturally release pressure. Open the lid with care.
10. Allow the turkey to rest for 5 minutes before removing.
11. Set turkey on a platter. Rest 20 minutes before slicing.
12. Serve.

Nutritional Information per serving:

Calories: 225, Fat: 15g, Carbohydrates: 0g, Dietary Fiber: 0g, Protein: 32g

86. Luscious Broccoli and Asparagus with Roasted Almonds

Time: 20 minutes

Servings: 4

Ingredients:

- 1 head broccoli, chopped into florets
- 1 pound asparagus, stemmed and chopped
- 4 garlic cloves, minced
- 1 cup almonds, chopped
- 2 Tablespoons coconut oil
- 1 shallot, thinly sliced
- 1 cup vegetable broth
- ¼ cup fresh parsley, chopped
- 1 teaspoon salt (to taste)
- 1 teaspoon fresh ground black pepper (to taste)

Instructions:

1. Press Sauté mode on Instant Pot. Heat the coconut oil.
2. Sauté shallots and garlic for 2 minutes. Add broccoli florets and asparagus. Cook until vegetables soften.
3. Add remaining ingredients. Stir well.
4. Close and seal lid. Press Manual button. Cook on high pressure for 15 minutes.
5. Quick-Release the pressure when done. Open the lid with care. Stir well.
6. Serve.

Nutritional Information per servings:

Calories: 60, Fat: 1g, Carbohydrates: 4g, Protein: 2g, and Dietary Fiber: 3g

87. Yummy Mango Puree

Time: 20 minutes

Servings: 4

Ingredients:

- 2 mangos, chopped
- ¼ cup plump golden raisins
- 1 shallot, chopped
- 1 Tablespoon coconut oil
- 1 apple, cored and chopped
- 1 teaspoon cinnamon
- 2 Tablespoons fresh ginger, minced
- 1 cup granulated Splenda
- 1 Tablespoon apple cider vinegar
- 2 cups of water

Instructions:

1. Press Sauté button on Instant Pot. Heat the coconut oil.
2. Sauté shallot and ginger until translucent.
3. Press Keep Warm/Cancel button to cancel Sauté mode.
4. Add remaining ingredients. Stir well.
5. Close and seal lid. Press Manual button. Cook at High Pressure for 7 minutes.
6. When the timer beeps, quick-release pressure. Open the lid with care. Stir ingredients.
7. Use immersion blender to blend ingredients until smooth.
8. Allow to cool in refrigerator.

Nutritional Information per serving:

Calories: 80, Fat: 0.5g, Dietary Fiber: 1g, Carbohydrates: 5g, Protein: 1g

88. Crunchy Pumpkin Pie

Time: 30 minutes

Servings: 6

Filling Ingredients:

- 3 cups pumpkin puree
- ½ cup granulated Splenda
- ½ cup coconut milk
- 2 teaspoons pumpkin pie spice
- 1 large egg

Crust Ingredients:

- 1 cup pecan cookies, crushed
- 1 cup toasted pecans, roughly chopped
- 2 Tablespoons ghee, melted

Instructions:

1. In a large bowl, combine pecan cookies and ghee.
2. In a separate bowl, combine filling ingredients.
3. Grease pie pan, suitable for Instant Pot, with non-stick cooking spray.
4. Firmly press crust mixture into bottom of pan.
5. Pour filling into crust. Top with toasted pecans. Cover with aluminum foil.
6. Pour 2 cups of water in Instant Pot. Place trivet in Pot. Place pie pan on the trivet.
7. Close and seal lid. Press Manual button. Cook at High Pressure for 15 minutes.
8. When the timer beeps, naturally release pressure. Open the lid with care.
9. Cool for 30 minutes on counter. Refrigerate remaining portion.

Nutritional Information per serving:

Calories: 215, Carbohydrates: 6g, Fat: 12g, Protein: 4g, Dietary Fiber: 2g

Chapter 9: Amazing Desserts

89. Delectable Brownie Cake

Time: 25 minutes

Servings: 6

Ingredients:

- 4 Tablespoons butter, softened
- 2 eggs
- 1 cup of water
- ⅛ teaspoon salt
- ⅓ cup coconut flour (or almond meal)
- ⅓ cup cocoa powder, unsweetened
- ⅓ cup granulated Splenda
- ⅓ cup dark chocolate chips
- ⅓ cup chopped nuts (optional)

Instructions:

1. In a bowl, combine butter, eggs, water, coconut flour, cocoa powder, salt, and granulated Splenda. Stir well, but don't overmix.
2. Grease a 6-inch pan, suitable for Instant Pot, with non-stick cooking spray.
3. Pour brownie mixture in pan. Cover with aluminum foil.
4. Pour water in Instant Pot. Place a trivet inside. Place cake pan on trivet.
5. Close and seal lid. Press Manual button. Cook at High Pressure for 20 minutes.
6. Release pressure naturally when done. Open the lid with care.
7. Remove pan from Instant Pot. Allow to cool 15 minutes before slicing.

Nutritional Information per serving:

Calories: 202, Fat: 20g, Protein: 4g, Carbohydrates, 7g, Dietary Fiber: 3g

90. Healthy Corn Pudding

Time: 20 minutes

Servings: 4

Ingredients:

- 2 (14-ounce) cans of creamed corn
- 2 cups of water
- 2 cups coconut milk
- 2 Tablespoons granulated Splenda
- 2 large eggs
- 2 Tablespoons coconut flour
- ⅛ teaspoon salt
- 1 Tablespoon butter, softened

Instructions:

1. Pour 2 cups of water in Instant Pot. Place trivet inside.
2. Set to Simmer. Bring to a boil.
3. In a bowl, combine creamed corn, coconut milk, Splenda, eggs, coconut flour, salt, and butter. Stir well.
4. Grease a baking dish, suitable for Instant Pot, with non-stick cooking spray.
5. Pour corn mixture in baking dish. Cover with aluminum foil.
6. Place baking dish on trivet.
7. Close and seal lid. Press Manual button. Cook on High Pressure for 20 minutes.
8. Quick-release or naturally release pressure when done. Open the lid with care.
9. Remove corn pudding. Allow to cool before serving.

Nutritional Information per serving:

Calories: 125, Fat: 5g, Protein: 9g, Carbohydrates: 12g, Dietary Fiber: 2g

91. Lovely Cinnamon Baked Apples

Time: 10 minutes

Servings: 4

Ingredients:

- 6 apples, cored and sliced (or chopped)
- ½ cup plump golden raisins
- ½ cup nuts, chopped (your choice)
- 1 teaspoon pure cinnamon powder
- 3 packets raw stevia
- 1 teaspoon apple pie spice
- 3 Tablespoons butter, softened

Instructions:

1. In your Instant Pot, combine apples, raisins, nuts, cinnamon powder, stevia, apple pie spice, and butter. Stir well.
2. Close and seal lid. Press Manual button. Cook at High Pressure for 10 minutes.
3. Release pressure naturally when done. Open the lid with care.
4. Serve.

Nutritional Information per serving:

Calories: 150, Carbohydrates: 15g, Fat: .05g, Protein: 0.5g, Dietary Fiber: 3.5g

92. Delicious Peach Cobbler

Time: 20 minutes

Servings: 4

Ingredients:

- 8 peaches, peeled and chopped
- 2 Tablespoons butter, softened
- ½ cup coconut flour
- 1 teaspoon vanilla extract
- ¼ cup granulated Splenda
- ¼ cup low-carb brown sugar
- 1 teaspoon pure cinnamon
- 1 teaspoon lime juice
- 1 cup coconut milk

Instructions:

1. In your Instant Pot, place peaches in single layer along bottom.
2. In a large bowl, combine coconut milk, butter, vanilla extract, coconut flour, brown sugar, and Splenda. Stir well. Pour mixture over peaches.
3. Close and seal lid. Press Manual button. Cook on High Pressure for 10 minutes.
4. Release pressure naturally when done. Open the lid with care.
5. Spoon into bowls.

Nutritional Information per Serving: Calories: 200, Carbohydrates: 20g, Protein: 5g, Fat: 6g, Dietary Fiber: 3g

93. Creamy Chocolate Pudding

Time: 20 minutes

Servings: 2

Ingredients:

- 1 cup organic coconut milk
- 1½ cups organic heavy cream
- 2 Tablespoons cocoa powder, unsweetened
- ½ teaspoon stevia powder extract
- 1 Tablespoons raw, organic honey
- 8-ounce bittersweet dark chocolate, chopped
- 2 large eggs
- 2 Tablespoons butter, softened
- ⅓ cup coconut flour
- ¼ cup granulated Splenda
- ⅓ cup low-carb brown sugar
- 2 teaspoons vanilla extract
- ¼ teaspoon cinnamon
- ⅛ teaspoon salt
- 2 Tablespoons of water

Instructions:

1. In a saucepan, add coconut milk, heavy cream, cocoa powder, stevia powder extract, and honey. Stir well. Simmer 3 minutes.
2. Remove saucepan from heat. Add dark chocolate. Stir until melted. Set aside. Let it cool slightly before adding to rest of mixture.
3. In a large bowl, combine eggs, coconut flour, brown sugar, Splenda, vanilla extract, cinnamon, butter, and salt. Stir well.
4. Add chocolate mixture to batter. Stir well.
5. Pour 2 cups of water in Instant Pot. Place trivet inside.
6. Grease a pan, suitable for Instant Pot, with non-stick cooking spray.
7. Pour batter in pan. Cover with aluminum foil. Place on trivet.
8. Close and seal lid. Press Manual button. Cook at High Pressure for 10 minutes.
9. Release pressure naturally when done. Open the lid with care.
10. Remove pan from Instant Pot. Allow to cool.
11. Serve.

Nutritional Information per serving:

Calories: 150, Carbohydrates: 5g, Protein: 5g, Fat: 7g, Dietary Fiber: 0g

94. Just as Filling Cauliflower Rice Pudding

Time: 20 minutes

Servings: 2

Ingredients:

- 1 head cauliflower
- 2 cups coconut milk
- 1 cup heavy cream
- 4 teaspoons cinnamon powder
- 1 teaspoon granulated Splenda
- 1 teaspoon pure stevia extract
- 1 teaspoon pure vanilla extract
- ½ teaspoon salt

Instructions:

1. Chop up cauliflower. Place pieces in food processor.
2. Pulse until cauliflower is rice-like consistency.
3. Pour cauliflower rice in Instant Pot.
4. Add coconut milk, cinnamon, Splenda, stevia extract, vanilla extract, and salt. Stir well.
5. Close and seal lid. Press Porridge button. Cook at High Pressure for 20 minutes.
6. When done, allow pressure to release naturally for 10 minutes.
7. After 10 minutes, press the Cancel button. Open the lid with care.
8. To finish off, add cream and vanilla extract. Stir well.
9. Serve in bowls.

Nutritional Information per serving:

Calories: 90, Fat: 3g, Carbohydrates: 5g, Protein: 8g, Dietary Fiber: 1g

95. Almost-Famous Chocolate Lava Cake

Time: 15 minutes

Servings: 4

Ingredients:

- ⅓ cup granulated Splenda
- 2 Tablespoons butter, softened
- ¼ cup coconut milk
- ¼ cup coconut flour (or any ketogenic alternatives)
- 1 large egg
- 1 Tablespoon cocoa powder, unsweetened
- Zest from ½ a lime
- ½ teaspoon baking powder
- ⅛ teaspoon salt
- 1 cup of water
- 4 ramekins

Instructions:

1. In a bowl, combine eggs, Splenda, butter, milk, coconut flour, egg, cocoa powder, lime zest, baking powder, and salt. Stir well.
2. Grease 4 ramekins with non-stick cooking spray.
3. Divide batter evenly in 4 ramekins.
4. Pour 2 cups of water in Instant Pot. Place trivet inside. Place ramekins on trivet.
5. Close and seal lid. Press Manual button. Cook at High Pressure for 7 minutes.
6. When done, allow pressure to release naturally. Remove ramekins.
7. Allow lava cakes to cool 5 minutes.
8. Serve.

Nutritional Information per serving:

Calories: 125, Fat: 4g, Carbohydrates: 20g, Protein: 2g, Dietary Fiber: 1g

96. Irresistible Lemon Cheesecake

Time: 30 minutes (plus 6 hours for refrigerating)   Servings: 4

Ingredients:

- 1½ cups low-carb graham crackers (approximately 10-12 crackers)
- 2 teaspoons low-carb brown sugar
- 2 Tablespoons butter, melted
- 1 Tablespoon almond flour
- 1 package (16-ounce) cream cheese, softened
- ½ cup granulated sugar
- 1 teaspoon vanilla extract
- 2 large eggs
- ½ cup heavy whipping cream
- Zest and juice from 1 lemon

Instructions:

1. In a food processor, add graham crackers, brown sugar, and butter.
2. Pulse until well blended, almost sand-like consistency.
3. Grease a 6-inch cheesecake pan with non-stick cooking spray.
4. Press crust mixture into bottom of pan firmly.
5. Place in freezer for 10 minutes to harden.
6. In a separate bowl, combine cream cheese, granulated sugar, heavy cream, eggs, almond flour, zest and juice from lemon, and vanilla extract.
7. Stir vigorously or blend with hand mixer until smooth.
8. Pour filling over crust. Cover cheesecake pan with aluminum foil.
9. Pour 2 cups of water in Instant Pot. Place trivet inside. Place pan on trivet.
10. Close and seal lid. Press Manual button. Cook at High Pressure for 20 minutes.
11. Once done, naturally release pressure. Open the lid with care.
12. Allow cheesecake to rest in Instant Pot for 20 minutes.
13. Transfer cheesecake to refrigerator. Cool for 6 hours or overnight.
14. Top with whip cream and fresh lemon zest when serving.

Nutritional Information per serving:

Calories: 170, Fat: 10g, Protein: 7g, Carbohydrates: 15g, Dietary Fiber: 0.4g

97. Berry Bliss Cheesecake

Time: 30 minutes (plus 6 hours for refrigerating)   Servings: 4

Ingredients:

- 1½ cups low-carb graham crackers (approximately 10-12 crackers)
- 1 Tablespoon granulated Splenda
- 4 Tablespoons butter, melted
- 2 packages (16-ounce) cream cheese, softened:
- 1 cup granulated Splenda
- 3 large eggs
- ¼ cup sour cream
- Zest and juice from 1 lemon
- 1 teaspoon vanilla extract
- 1 cup heavy whipping cream
- 4 cups mixed fresh berries (keto-friendly, your choice)

Instructions:

1. Mash half the berries with a fork. Set aside.
2. In a food processor, add graham crackers, granulated Splenda, melted butter.
3. Pulse until sand-like consistency.
4. Grease 6-inch cheesecake pan, to fit Instant Pot, with non-stick cooking spray.
5. Press crust mixture into bottom of pan. Place in freezer 10 minutes to harden.
6. In a separate bowl, combine cream cheese, Splenda, eggs, sour cream, zest and juice from lemon, vanilla and heavy cream. Add crushed mixed berries.
7. Stir vigorously or blend with hand mixer until smooth.
8. Pour mixture over crust. Cover cheesecake pan with aluminum foil.
9. Pour 2 cups of water in Instant Pot. Place trivet inside. Place pan on trivet.
10. Close and seal lid. Press Manual button. Cook at High Pressure for 20 minutes.
11. Once done, naturally release pressure. Open the lid with care.
12. Allow cheesecake to rest for 20 minutes in Instant Pot.
13. Transfer cheesecake to refrigerator. Cool for 6 hours or overnight.
14. Top with rest of fresh berries when serving.

Nutritional Information per serving:

Calories: 200, Fat: 20g, Carbohydrates: 20g, Dietary Fiber: 2g, Protein: 6g

98. Fantastic Bread Pudding

Time: 25 minutes

Servings: 4

Ingredients:

- 6 slices low-carb day-old/stale bread, cut into cubes
- 1½ cups unsweetened almond milk
- 4 Tablespoons unsalted butter
- 3 large eggs
- ¼ cup granulated Splenda
- ¾ cup low-carb dark chocolate chips
- 1 teaspoon vanilla extract
- 1 cup plump golden raisins
- Zest from 1 lemon
- 2 cups of water

Instructions:

1. In a small bowl, combine eggs, Splenda and almond milk. Whisk until combined.
2. Melt the butter.
3. In a large bowl, add the bread. Pour melted butter over bread.
4. Add lemon zest, chocolate chips, and raisins.
5. Pour liquid mixture over bread. Stir well.
6. Grease baking dish, to fit Instant Pot, with non-stick cooking spray.
7. Pour in bread mixture. Cover with aluminum foil.
8. Pour 2 cups of water in Instant Pot. Place trivet inside. Place dish on trivet.
9. Close and seal lid. Press Manual button. Cook at High Pressure for 20 minutes.
10. Release pressure naturally when done. Open the lid with care.
11. Allow bread pudding to rest 15 minutes in Instant Pot.
12. Serve.

Nutritional Information per Serving:

Calories: 200, Fat: 7g, Dietary Fiber: 2g, Carbohydrates: 20g, Protein: 10g

Chapter 10: Wicked Recipes

99. Fabulous Goose Meat

Time: 30 minutes

Servings: 4

Ingredients:

- 4 goose breasts, boneless, skinless (or any other goose meat)
- 1 (12-ounce) can cream of mushroom soup
- 2 Tablespoons coconut oil
- 1 teaspoon garlic powder
- 1 teaspoon onion powder
- 1 teaspoon paprika
- 2 teaspoons salt
- 2 teaspoons fresh ground black pepper

Instructions:

1. Press Sauté button on Instant Pot. Heat the coconut oil.
2. Sauté goose meat until golden brown crust per side.
3. Press Keep Warm/Cancel button to end Sauté mode.
4. In a small bowl, combine the spices. Sprinkle the seasoning over the goose.
5. Pour cream of mushroom soup over meat.
6. Close and seal lid. Press Manual button. Cook at High Pressure for 10 minutes.
7. When the timer beeps, naturally release pressure. Open the lid with care.
8. Allow dish to rest 5 minutes before removing from Instant Pot.
9. Serve.

Nutritional Information per serving:

Calories: 300, Fat: 8g, Dietary Fiber: 1g, Carbohydrates: 1g, Protein 30g

100. Nourishing Jambalaya

Time: 15 minutes

Servings: 4

Ingredients:

- 1 pound chicken breasts, boneless, skinless
- 1 pound Italian sausage
- 2 Tablespoons coconut oil
- 1 red onion, chopped
- 2 garlic cloves, minced
- 2 cups cauliflower rice
- 2 bell peppers, chopped
- 2 cups crushed tomatoes
- 1 Tablespoon Worcestershire sauce
- 3 cups chicken broth
- 1 teaspoon salt (to taste)
- 1 teaspoon fresh ground black pepper (to taste)

Instructions:

1. Rinse the chicken, pat dry. Chop into bite-size pieces.
2. Slice Italian sausage into circles, ¼ inch thick.
3. Press Sauté button on Instant Pot. Heat the coconut oil,
4. Sauté red onion and garlic for 2 minutes.
5. Add chicken and Italian sausage. Sauté until meat is brown.
6. Press Keep Warm/Cancel to end Sauté mode.
7. Add cauliflower rice, bell peppers, crushed tomatoes. Stir well.
8. Stir in chicken broth, Worcestershire sauce, salt and pepper.
9. Close and seal lid. Press Manual button. Cook at High Pressure for 10 minutes.
10. Quick-Release the pressure when done. Open the lid with care.
11. Serve.

Nutritional Information per servings:

Calories: 250, Fat: 15g, Dietary Fiber: 1g, Carbohydrates: 11g, Protein: 30g

101. Party Octopus

Time: 20 minutes

Servings: 4

Ingredients:

- 1 octopus, cleaned
- 2 Tablespoons ghee, melted
- Juice from ½ lemon
- 1 Tablespoon fresh rosemary, chopped
- 1 Tablespoon fresh oregano, chopped
- 1 Tablespoon of fresh thyme, chopped
- 1 teaspoon garlic powder
- 1 teaspoon onion powder
- 1 teaspoon salt
- 1 teaspoon fresh ground black pepper
- 2 cups of water

Instructions:

1. Place octopus in Instant Pot.
2. Add melted ghee, water, lemon juice, herbs, and seasonings. Stir well.
3. Close and seal lid. Pres Manual button. Cook at High Pressure for 15 minutes.
4. When the timer beeps, naturally release pressure. Open the lid with care.
5. Serve.

Nutritional Information per serving:

Calories: 175, Fat: 3g, Dietary Fiber: 0g, Carbohydrates: 0g, Protein: 9g

Conclusion

We appreciate you selecting this Instant Pot Cookbook!

After reading this book, you will understand what the Instant Pot is, why it is good for you, and how to use it. You are now prepared to embark on the Instant Pot Cooking Lifestyle with 101 recipes.

Thank you and the best of blessings!

Made in the USA
San Bernardino, CA
07 June 2018